To Gerry, it's about time.

Credits

25, 31–32, 38: © 2012 Marc Prensky; 29: Lee Jenkins, author. *Permission to Forget: And Nine Other Root Causes of America's Frustration with Education*; 52, 53: James Bond/Liz Anderson; 55, 56, 57, 58, 61, 62, 67: Reprinted with the permission of Simon & Schuster, Inc., from STEVE JOBS by Walter Isaacson. Copyright © 2011 by Walter Isaacson. All rights reserved. From STEVE JOBS by Walter Isaacson. Copyright © 2011 by Walter Isaacson. Reproduced with permission by Little, Brown Book Group; 59–60: Courtesy David Booth.

Stratosphere

Integrating Technology, Pedagogy, and Change Knowledge

Michael Fullan

Feedback on this publication can be sent to editorialfeedback@pearsoned.com.

Pearson Canada Inc.
26 Prince Andrew Place
Don Mills, ON M3C 2T8
Customer Service: 1-800-361-6128

Published simultaneously in Canada (www.pearsoncanada.ca) and the United States (www.pearsoned.com)

6   16
Printed and bound in the United States

Vice-President, Publishing: Mark Cobham
Research and Communications Manager: Chris Allen
Managing Editor: Joanne Close
Project Editor: Lisa Dimson
Copy Editor: Kate Revington
Proofreader: Tilman Lewis
Indexer: Noeline Bridge
Permissions Editor: Christina Beamish
Production Coordinator: Susan Wong
Cover Image: © Kris Hanke
Composition: Lapiz Digital Services
Manufacturing Coordinator: Karen Bradley

ISBN: 978-0-13-248314-8

Contents

Acknowledgments

Thanks to my numerous friends and colleagues with whom we mix and match on so many great projects. To Claudia Cuttress, who supports me in all of our endeavors, and to Eleanor Adam, Liz Anderson, James Bond, David Booth, Carol Campbell, Katelyn Donnelly, Mary Jean Gallagher, Andy Hargreaves, Peter Hill, David Hopkins, Brendan Kelly, Maria Langworthy, Ken Leithwood, Tony MacKay, Steve Munby, Charles Pascal, Joanne Quinn, Carol Rolheiser, Geoff Scott, and Nancy Watson.

Multi-faceted thanks to the Motion Leadership/Madcap (MLM) team with whom I am working. To my partner in this endeavor, David Devine, and to Greg Butler, Claudia Cuttress again, Mark Hand, Richard Mozer, Lyn Sharratt, Bill Hogarth, Malcolm Clarke, and to all of the curriculum, writing, and digital creators who work with us. To our three great advisors and friends, Sir Michael Barber, Sir Ken Robinson, and Peter Senge. In MLM we are endeavoring to create a powerful learning product through the development of digital curriculum innovations aligned with the Common Core State Standards in the United States and backed up by a teacher-implementation support system for whole-system reform.

To my two favorite politicians: Ontario Premier Dalton McGuinty and former minister of education, Gerard Kennedy.

To my family: Wendy, Bailey, and Conor, who enable all of us to live in some kind of ideal world.

To the great publishing team at Pearson Canada: Marty Keast, Mark Cobham, Joanne Close, Lisa Dimson, and Kate Revington—so great to work with—thanks for getting this work out, combining speed with quality.

Here's to a better stratospheric world: 64 kilometers deep and 40,000 kilometers wide, and more if you want to get seriously extraterrestrial.

About the Author

Michael Fullan is Professor Emeritus at the Ontario Institute for Studies in Education, University of Toronto, and Special Advisor on Education to the Premier of Ontario, Dalton McGuinty. He works in Ontario and around the world on accomplishing whole-system reform in provinces, states, and countries. He has received several honorary doctorates. His award-winning books have been published in many languages. Recent titles include *Motion Leadership, Change Leader, Putting FACES on the Data* (with Lyn Sharratt), and *Professional Capital: Transforming Teaching in Every School* (with Andy Hargreaves).

Visit his website at www.michaelfullan.ca.

Preface

In the original edition of *Stratosphere* I wrote, "We are at the early stages of a potentially powerful confluence of factors that could transform education." In some ways I was reading the tea leaves. There was evidence that students and teachers were becoming increasingly bored by traditional schooling as they moved up the grades. At the same time, there were some powerful emergent forces not yet connected—technology, pedagogy, and change knowledge.

Technology, or digital innovation, was developing wildly and was evident almost everywhere but in our schools. And when it did appear there, it seemed to be driven primarily by an acquisition mentality: buy it because it is the wave of the future. As a consequence, superficial or non-use was the norm for these digital aids. Pedagogy or instruction was, of course, part and parcel of the boredom. By and large, students were not engaged in their own learning. Given that we are talking about the teaching profession, it was strange that there was no systematic focus on continuously improving instruction. Finally, change knowledge, my own field, was mired in what I considered the wrong policy drivers—external accountability, individualism, technology acquisition, and ad hoc policies.[1]

But there was something different that I could sense in early 2013. The three powerful dormant forces were beginning to connect in almost natural and inevitable ways. I began to see this phenomenon in regular schools—for example, W.G. Davis a senior public school in Ontario with principal Andreas Meyer and his teachers (see www.michaelfullan .ca, YouTube.ca). Such schools seem to be coming out of the woodwork. There was no overt external help provided; they just did it! They focused on pedagogy as a foundation (learning partnerships between and among teachers and students); they added and integrated technology to accelerate and deepen learning; and they employed the skills of change leadership (build capacity, use the group [purposeful collaboration], link pedagogy to learning outcomes, persist without being negative).

Once I saw that social media and other network learning would rapidly spread and connect ideas—ideas that garnered instant, natural interest—I was certain that this learning revolution could take off. Unlike previous innovations it was something that had to be more enabled than forced. This is the work that my colleagues and I have been engaged in since the publication of *Stratosphere*, work that goes much beyond what we are doing (after all, it is a learning revolution). Maria Langworthy and I framed this work in our report *A Rich Seam: How New Pedagogies Find Deep Learning.*[2]

Then we moved to action, creating a global learning network of clusters of schools who wanted to work together and with us on what we call "New pedagogies for deep learning" (www.npdl.global). Currently, there are over 600 schools in 7 different countries involved in innovating and implementing deep learning. They have joined because they were or wanted to move into what I will call the stratosphere domain of action. We have created a framework to guide this work that consists of five components. Working backward from outcomes the framework includes:

  i) deep learning outcomes (character education, citizenship, collaboration, communication, creativity, and critical thinking);

  ii) new pedagogies (learning partnerships between and among teachers, students, and parents);

  iii) school conditions;

  iv) district or regional factors; and

  v) policy and infrastructure.

You can track our development on the website, in addition to the considerable publications and video that we will disseminate. We see our work as part and parcel of the transformation that I identified in *Stratosphere*.

Alongside this work is the broader capacity building initiatives that we are engaged in in several jurisdictions, in particular, Ontario, California, and New Zealand.[3] In all these cases, the focus is on whole systems (the entire state, province, or country), pedagogical transformation (new learning partnerships), linked to deep learning outcomes (the 6Cs above). For all parties there is an increased agency and partnership with others: students, teachers, parents and community, and administrators and policy makers.

I have to say that this is the most exciting change movement that I have been part of. It is exciting but also challenging because there are many innovations to consider and assess, and we are talking about *whole system transformation*. Read or re-read *Stratosphere* and you will appreciate the origins of these developments, and speculate about where they might be heading. There are resistant forces, preferring the current system remain unchanged. I predict that the next decade will be witness to a tug of war between the status quo and what I would call the new and relentless forces of the stratosphere trio of technology, pedagogy, and change knowledge. This is your chance to make yourself part of the action and learn from as well as contribute to the movement as a whole.

Michael Fullan
August 2015

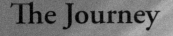

The Journey

Three big ideas have needed each other for more than 40 years without knowing it. They are technology, especially since the first personal computers surfaced almost a half a century ago; pedagogy, especially since universal high-school education became a goal in the mid-1960s; and change knowledge, especially since implementation became the worry around 1970. These three forces have now developed to the point that powerful synergy with fantastic results for learning is in the offing.

I call this triad "the stratosphere." It is bigger than the cloud—it is a vast source of internet resources "out there," its physical location unknown. But it does exist, and we are able to access it from our mobile devices. The cloud is out there and in here simultaneously. We don't need to understand it to appreciate it. Stratosphere is like that, only more sublime. It includes technology with its huge, ever expanding storehouses of information, but also opportunities to learn differently, what I call pedagogy; and it incorporates change knowledge—what we should do with all this information to change things, presumably for the better.

I won't say that these three forces—technology, pedagogy, and change knowledge—intentionally seek one another out in the stratosphere, but I can say that it is inevitable that they connect. This book is about making that connection more explicit and more beneficial for humankind. The term *stratosphere* is intended to connote mystery, intrigue, and unknowns. It also includes mysteries that we cannot comprehend, such as new research that the brain unconsciously forms meaningful relationships not only with other humans, but also with seemingly inanimate things. It makes the inanimate human, if you like. Iain McGilchrist's *The Master and His Emissary: The Divided Brain and the Making of the Western World* is a prodigious investigation of the fathoms of the brain in relation to the universe.[1] McGilchrist argues that what we pay attention to not only interprets the world but *alters it and in so doing, alters us.*

Allow a little mystery here. For us truly to experience something, says McGilchrist, "it has to enter into and alter us, and there must be something in us which specifically responds to it as unique." This is most clearly seen in relation to art. A great work of art, according to McGilchrist, is "more like a living being than a thing. That our encounter with that being matters and means something depends on the fact that any living being is itself whole and coherent, and forms part of a larger context in which we too are involved and engaged."[2] In effect, stratosphere says that a great piece of technology is like a living being *because of the way we experience it.* This is why I say later, not all that whimsically, that in the not-too-distant future, some of us may be marrying our robots. Don't worry, we will get very concrete in this book, but I want to hold out at the outset the mystery of humanity and its universe—a mystery that technology only amplifies. One last abstraction: Listen to McGilchrist talk about the left and right hemispheres of the brain:

> The left hemisphere is always engaged in a *purpose*: it always has an end in view, and downgrades whatever has no instrumental purpose in sight. The right hemisphere, by contrast, has no designs on anything. It is vigilant for whatever *is* without preconceptions, without a defined purpose… The world of the left hemisphere, dependent on denotative language and abstraction, yields clarity and power to manipulate things that are known, fixed, static, isolated, decontextualized, explicit, disembodied, general in nature, but ultimately lifeless. The right hemisphere, by contrast, yields a world of individual, changing, evolving, interconnected, implicit, incarnate, living beings within the context of the lived world, but in the nature of things never fully graspable, always imperfectly known—and to this world it exists in a relationship of care.[3]

I can't imagine a more profound critique of how the current education system is so very inappropriately content bound and why the new pedagogy—learning how to learn—is so essential. Learn how to learn because the evolving world is ever changing and elusive. We need the capacity to keep up—to periodically grasp the ungraspable. Only those who know how to learn, who can relate to others *and* the environment (including "things"), and who make the world part of their own evolving being will thrive in this world. It is damn exciting to live in the world with the brain we have.

This book is about how the ideas embedded in the new technology, the new pedagogy, and the new change knowledge are converging to transform education for all. I have worked on two of these three matters for some time, attempting to integrate good instructional practices with what we call "whole-system reform"—the moral purpose of raising the bar and closing the gap for *all* students in the entire state, province, or country. We have not gone far enough in promoting the new pedagogy—learning how to learn—and this is where technology comes into play. Technology has had its own pace, wildly outstripping the other two in sheer quantity and in aimless quality. It is now time to reconcile how technology can join the fray in a more purposeful way in order to transform learning for educators and learners in the 21st century.

For change connoisseurs such as myself, nirvana is how to make change *easier*. Change will become more enjoyable when it proffers experiences that are engaging, precise, and specific; high yield (good benefit relative to effort); higher order (stretching humans in creativity, problem solving, and innovation); and collaborative for individual and collective benefit. We have these four elements now, but not at scale. The good news is that they have become clearer in the past year or two, along with research evidence to prove their worth.

We have had good success in accomplishing whole-system reform in Ontario. Since 2003, we have taken a stagnant system and made impressive gains across the 5,000 schools in the public education system. Literacy and numeracy, deeply defined, have increased by 15 percent in the 4,000 elementary schools; high-school graduation rates have climbed to 82 percent from 68 percent and are still on the rise. Morale, capacity, and ownership have become embedded in the schools, districts, and government agencies. Technology has not played much of a role to this point, which could explain why top-end higher-order skills have not moved much, remaining at about 13 percent of the school population, according to the assessment of the provincial agency Education Quality and Accountability Office (EQAO).

Research on pedagogy is now demonstrating that even for higher-order skills, small investments in targeted relationships with students pay off with high-yield motivational and achievement results. Technology can accelerate these learning experiences on a large scale with minimal costs after initial investments. In subsequent chapters, we will flesh out what the new pedagogy means and give precision to the vague phrase that we need to "flip the roles of teacher and student."

We are learning more about large-scale change, making it less complicated by focusing on a small number of ambitious goals with a coherent strategy that attends in concert to half a dozen or so key factors: intrinsic motivation, capacity building, transparency of results and practice, leadership at all levels, and a positive but assertive stance on progress. Borrowing from Jeff Kluger, I call this change knowledge "simplexity"—a small number of key factors (the simple part) that must be made to gel with large groups of people (the complex aspect).

We will see that there are huge dangers of technology making matters worse for humankind. We will also discover that we can learn to live in the cloud with increasing clarity and excitement of purpose and learning. Although we are at the very early stages of this convergence, we can point to its specific nature and manifestations. We can comfortably predict that once this phenomenon becomes clearer, as is the main purpose of this book, it will accelerate. It will, if you like, go viral. We will want to know how to cope with this new viral world and to maximize our capacity to turn it to our advantage.

In *Stratosphere,* as we shall see, I hold out four criteria for integrating technology and pedagogy to produce exciting, innovative learning experiences for *all* students—something desperately needed to bring education into the 21st century. These new developments must be i) irresistibly engaging (for students and for teachers); ii) elegantly efficient and easy to use; iii) technologically ubiquitous 24/7; and iv) steeped in real-life problem solving. Currently, some ad hoc examples in practice can give us glimpses of what these experiences might look like, but these are rarities.

The real revolution that I take up in this book makes sustained learning experiences a reality for all students. Integrating technology, pedagogy, and change knowledge is fundamentally liberating. It democratizes learning so that every student learns how to learn for a lifetime of pursuing personal passion, purpose, and fulfillment. Best of all, students learn collaboratively, consolidating connections with others locally and from afar. Citizenship, human solidarity, collective problem-solving, and sustainability are thereby served.

More than this, our change knowledge about how to accomplish whole-system reform is becoming increasingly specific and clear.

We know more about how to engage diverse people in processes of deep improvement that generate ownership and establish conditions for continuous improvement. What makes this revolution real, not hypothetical, is that changes in technology and pedagogy are also becoming dramatically compelling. Essentially, the case in *Stratosphere* is that the trio of technology, pedagogy, and change knowledge makes for an unbeatable combination. The convergence is so strong that we may well see in the immediate future multiple lines of breakthrough solutions radicalizing how and what we learn. Education and technology BFF!

In education we have just about reached the end of squeezing good out of an outdated school system. The current system is too costly, too ineffective, and as any kid will tell you, deadly boring. This can be changed and it will turn out to be easier than we think—easier because the new alternatives are incredibly less expensive and immensely more engaging. This is the journey of *Stratosphere*, from understanding the powers and perils of technology, to carving out easier and more effective change, to using our change knowledge to establish a new self-generating system of learning for all.

Technology: Power and Peril

When my friends and I built the first virtual reality machines, the whole point was to make this world more creative, expressive, empathic, and interesting. It was not to escape it.
—*Jaron Lanier*

Charles Darwin, late in life, wrote the following in a letter to a friend:

Up to the age of thirty, or beyond it, poetry of many kinds, such as the works of Milton, Gray, Byron, Wordsworth, Coleridge, and Shelley, gave me great pleasure... But now for many years I cannot endure to read a line of poetry... My mind seems to have become a kind of machine for grinding general laws out of large collections of facts...

And if I had to live my life again, I would have made a rule to read some poetry and listen to some music at least once every week... The loss of these tastes is a loss of happiness, and may possibly be injurious to the intellect, and more probably to the moral character, by enfeebling the emotional part of our nature.[1]

Could it be that the current generation of digital natives, the first to experience the full brunt of novel, prodigious technology, will sit down at the age of 100 one day and wonder about the loss of happiness that could have been and their enfeebled emotional nature? Even though technology will become even more marvelous with its seemingly endless possibilities, for the first time we live in a period where we can grasp how phenomenal our world has become. We now are in a position to wonder where it is going, to question its power for better or worse, and to then work together to begin turning it to our advantage. *Stratosphere* is about opening our eyes to both the dark side of technology and to its virtually unlimited enlightenment side—no powerful tool is ever neutral in its use.

The Dark Side of Technology

Is technology liberating or sinister? The answer is both, but we tend to be in awe of its magical powers, missing its hidden underside. Several of the techno pioneers, those most steeped in creating our current digital world, now want to disabuse us of the idea that technology is simply marvelous. It is with growing horror that one reads what these experts are worrying about.

For starters, take Evgeny Morozov's *The Net Delusion: The Dark Side of Internet Freedom*. His premise is that "the naïve belief that the Internet favors the oppressed rather than the oppressor is marred by what I call cyber-utopianism: a naïve belief in the emancipatory nature of online communication that rests on a stubborn refusal to acknowledge its downside."[2] Morozov proceeds to demonstrate that the web can strengthen rather than undermine authoritarian regimes (we not only know where you live, but who you are, what you like, where you like to do it, and so on). Morozov quotes Langdon Winner's ominous observation: "although virtually limitless in their power, our technologies are tools without handles."[3] (Later I will argue that we need to supply our own handles which can be for better or worse, with evolution favoring the former.)

Who works harder for their cause—authoritarians or libertarians? Not worth answering in a comprehensive sense, but the fascists can be thankful that the entertainment value of the internet easily outweighs the drive for political knowledge. In other words, it is more addictive to play Words with Friends than to attend a political rally, to try to figure out what is happening in the Middle East, or to listen to boring news. Morozov quotes Michael Anti, a Beijing-based expert on the Chinese internet, to the effect that in 2009 when the government lifted the ban on online pornography, they must have reasoned: "if Internet users have some porn to look at, then they won't pay so much attention to political matters."[4] In our education reform work, we even have a category, "beware of distractors"—factors and forces that divert people from maintaining focus on core priorities. Humankind is easily distracted, and all the more so when peers are egging one on.

Distraction, then, might be the best diversion for authoritarian governments because, as Morozov says, "controlling people through entertainment is cheaper and doesn't involve as much brutality."[5] Blatant policing drives people to dissent; easy entertainment either addles the mind or sharpens it for no purpose. We could go on, but the point is that, on the surface, the internet provides access to all while masking "the sophistication and flexibility of the censorship apparatus built on top of the Internet."[6] You can blog away to your friends and potential allies, while more purposeful enemies keep an eye on you.

For every initiative that seeks to use social networking for civic engagement and other democratic developments, there is somebody watching who does not value these priorities. There is much more to be done on the ground as we have found in our own social change work: focus, relentless discipline, continuous processing of data and problem solving, incorporation of newcomers, and so on. Internet participation in a social cause can easily be mistaken for doing something. Essentially, argues Morozov, the internet aids and abets shallow commitment.

Not just politics benefits from open access to information about us. Anyone with a vested interest can make our faces and personalities more visible without our knowing it and use the information in highly sophisticated ways to take advantage of or shape our behavior. Consider Eli Pariser's *filter bubble*. In *The Filter Bubble*, Pariser identifies one turning point as December 4, 2009, when Google quietly announced on its blog a commitment to personalized search for everyone. Google would use 57 signals to learn many things about us—where we were logging in from, what was our history of searches, what kinds of people we might be, what we might like—and point us to it in not so subtle ways. Says Pariser, "Democracy requires citizens to see things from one another's point of view, but instead we're more and more enclosed in our own bubbles."[7] The filter bubble is driven by search engines constantly figuring out and projecting who we are (or who we should want to be). Pariser quotes Eric Schmidt of Google who says customers want Google "to tell them what they should be doing next."[8] The internet is happy to construct our worlds through extrapolation, perhaps telling us when we will want our next slice of pizza and what we will want on it. According to Pariser, "a world constructed from the familiar is a world in which there is little to learn."[9]

It is not only that our learning can become more limited, but that the hidden world of information (not so hidden to those who can access it) is becoming downright sinister. In the February 4, 2012, edition of the *New York Times*, Somini Sengupta and Lori Andrews, in separate articles, both offer some examples of access to and use of information that are as chilling as they are believable. A student in Austria, for example, requested his own Facebook file which turned out to be 1,222 pages that contained old messages he had deleted, including some about a friend's troubled state of mind, and even information he didn't enter himself about his physical whereabouts.[10] In other words, if you use Google to do searches on a particular medical condition (which of us hasn't) or to find a summer camp for your child, you may soon see online advertisements that reflect these searches. Helpful or unsettling?

In Andrews' article "Facebook Is Using You," she points out that data aggregators can now group you according to interests, likes, and dislikes you share with others. Andrews details the example of one Atlanta man who, after returning from his honeymoon, discovered that American Express had lowered his credit limit by $7,000, not because of his personal credit history but rather because of where he had recently used his American Express card. In this instance, Andrews points out, the credit adjustment was made on the basis of aggregate data. The company's response left little doubt about why they decreased his limit. "Other customers who have used their card at establishments where you recently shopped have a poor repayment history with American Express." As Andrews comments, you might be refused health insurance based on a Google search you did about a medical condition. More ominous: if you are a young person who lives in a poor neighborhood, you are far more likely to see ads for trade schools than colleges.[11]

In short, we are being passively labeled and manipulated as if we were stooges in a psychology experiment. But we are in no hypothetical trial. In our everyday lives, we are being smothered and directed in ways that treat us as ignorant about our own futures. What makes for improvement is informed and committed action. For that you need information, dialogue, and the development of social capital based on mutual allegiance and skilled teamwork. Personalization should not mean directing us to the flavor of the month, at best putting us into contact with others like us, at worst determining our lives without our knowledge.

More critics—many of them pioneering technophiles—say that our brains are being distorted into a permanent state of hyper-distractionism. In *The Shallows: What the Internet Is Doing to Our Brains*, Nicholas Carr talks about what internet use is doing to *his* brain. Marshall McLuhan said we shape our tools and then they shape us. Carr is beginning to see what he meant. He is his own first-hand observer that he has lost all ability to concentrate: "what the Net seems to be doing is chipping away my capacity for concentration and contemplation."[12] In real time, Carr notes that his attention starts to drift after a page or two: "I get fidgety, lose the thread, begin looking for something else to do."[13] Carr basically says that his brain is constantly hungry for something, *any* something, independent of what he might have wanted.

Although hard to believe that our brains can be re-shaped in short order, given that evolution took millions of years, there does seem to be some evidence of plasticity, "the brain that changes itself," as Norman Doidge puts it.[14] Consider London cab drivers who historically have studied the streets of London in order to pass the eligibility exam, called "the knowledge," as they master the location of the city's more than 25,000 streets. Recent studies show that the shape of the brains of London cab drivers alters when they go from "the knowledge" to the use of a GPS; so apparently do our brains change as we go digital. Carr worries (his claim backed by dozens of studies) that we are moving away from the capacity for in-depth thinking where "when we go online, we enter an environment that promotes cursory reading, hurried and distracted thinking, and superficial learning."[15]

On the other hand, we know that some forms of digital engagement, such as video games, can be completely absorbing to the point that we forget to eat. (One addicted person I heard about kept a bottle by his computer so that he would not have to leave his time-sensitive game to urinate.) Our stratosphere world will have to be one where focus and immersion are for worthwhile endeavors. We do want to create a digital world where learners are *rapt*—"completely absorbed, engrossed, fascinated, perhaps even carried away" in experiences that are important for personal and group goals.[16]

We hear a lot about multi-taskers being poor at many different things—"multi-taskers are suckers for irrelevancy," says Clifford Nass[17]; people who read linear texts remember more and learn more than those who read things peppered with links and so on. But let me get a bit ahead of myself by saying we must remember that technology is evolving at an incredible rate so we should be careful about generalizing—it is different today than it was yesterday. And as we shall see, new forms of technology and new designs of use can serve our human and social needs much more effectively in the immediate future.

Meanwhile "the distractor lobby" is distracting us, a good thing because it will force us to consider how technology can help us focus and become deeply engaged, for example, in learning. One more piece: Maggie Jackson is so worried about us becoming permanently distracted that she subtitles her book *Distracted* "The Erosion of Attention and the Coming Dark Age"! Jackson's premise is simple: "The way we live is eroding our capacity for deep, sustained, perceptive attention—the building block of intimacy, wisdom, and cultural progress."[18] We are losing our focus, judgment, and awareness as humans and that, Jackson says, will be our demise.

Technology and Humans Shape Each Other

Enough doom and gloom. McLuhan was only partially right. We do shape our tools and then they *initially* shape us, but the relationship doesn't have to stay that way. It can be altered into a two-way street. Clay Shirky talks about the "milkshake mistake" made when McDonald's did some research on how to improve its milkshake. All but one researcher focused on how to improve milkshake content. The one researcher focused on when people bought milkshakes and discovered a whole new 8 a.m. crowd that wanted milkshakes because they were tasty, filling, and easy to consume. Basically, this researcher asked, "What job is a customer hiring a milkshake to do at 8 a.m.?"

Shirky said he made the same mistake in the 1990s when he focused directly on the capabilities of computers and the internet "with too little regard for the way human desires shape them."[19] Therein lies the beginning of our answer to reversing the trend of the dark side of technology holding sway. Don't focus on technology—focus on *its use*.

Kevin Kelly takes us a step closer when he discusses this intriguing question: What does technology want? First, Kelly wants us to be more proactive in relation to technology: "When we spy our technological fate in the distance, we should not reel back in horror of its inevitability; rather, we should lurch forward in preparation."[20] Noting the duality of its role, Kelly says that "humans are both master and slave to the *technium*" (the generic term he uses for technology).[21] Our fate and future is to realize that we will always be in this uncomfortable dual role: ever appreciative and ever alert to the pros and cons of specific technology usages.

In other words, it's not the milkshake—it's the customer! The future of technology boils down to humans. We should focus, as I do in this book, on what we, as humans, want technology to do. Realizing that there will always be bad guys with selfish and hateful motives, the fact is that the evolution of humankind favors pro-social behavior and collaboration: see David Sloan Wilson's *Evolution for Everyone*,[22] part of a body of literature too voluminous to review here. Technology in its evolution is not simply neutral; it can be shaped by what we want out of it. It does have a life of its own in that its growth is inevitable. What we must do then is constantly work on the matter of how to work *with* machines, not *against* them, and not in ignorance of them.

In complexity theory, the evolution of artifacts and the evolution of humans move along parallel paths that make positive convergence likely along the way, always accompanied by problematic possibilities. That is why we have to be alert to what we want and how to get it with technology's participation. Kelly observes, "Yes, technology is acquiring its own autonomy and will increasingly maximize its own agenda, but this agenda includes—as its foremost consequence—maximizing possibilities for us."[23] This is why Kelly eventually answers his question by concluding that "technology wants what life wants":

- Increasing efficiency
- Increasing opportunity
- Increasing emergence
- Increasing complexity
- Increasing diversity
- Increasing specialization
- Increasing ubiquity
- Increasing freedom
- Increasing mutualism
- Increasing beauty
- Increasing sentience
- Increasing structure
- Increasing evolvability[24]

When we turn these thoughts to technology and education, we have a long way to go. Technology in schooling has its dark side, including cyberbullying and inappropriate sexting, but its biggest problem is that it isn't present much. The digital life of students is largely outside schools, and it is a fairly undisciplined world, recalling worries of our distractor critics who see superficiality and long-term diminution of the brain as problems. Claudia Goldin and Lawrence Katz give us chapter and verse on what they call "the race between education and technology" in the United States.[25] You won't need any help guessing which is winning. Up until 1980 the United States led the world in education and in declining inequality. For the past 30 years U.S. education performance has steadily declined (now, depending on what measures of student achievement are used, it is currently about 25th in the world). Meanwhile, inequality in the United States has been increasing.

Goldin and Katz conclude that "technology has been racing ahead of education in recent decades because educational growth has been sluggish, not because skill-biased technical change has accelerated."[26] Try this for a crossover observation: technology has not raced ahead *inside schools*. Our answer in this book will not be let's load up technology in schools—I call this a "wrong driver"[27]—but rather, let's rethink how technology can be used at our service as well as push us to do even more.

Larry Rosen has described how out of touch schools are with the iGeneration. Children today hate school, he says, because they learn very differently than the way school teaches them. Armed with a lot of quantitative data, Rosen is perhaps too generous in his admiration of the iGeneration who, according to him, are introduced to technology at birth, are adept at multi-tasking, love virtual social worlds, and are confident and open to change.

But he is right about the constant media diet. He presents one chart that shows the hours and minutes per day that children use different media: 2:35 hours per day for children 6 months to 3 years old; 9:46 hours per day for children 9 to 12 years old; and 20:20 hours per day for young people 16 to 18 years old.[28] There are only so many hours in the day so presumably all are multi-tasking, including or maybe especially the babies.

Rosen begins to predict our *Stratosphere* model when he argues, "Smart educational models must consider social networks as a valuable source for enhancing student interest and participation in the classroom [our model includes participation outside the classroom as well]… The trick is to leverage their love of social networks to create educational tools built around them."[29]

It is revealing that Rosen takes a dramatically more sober position in his newest book (presumably because the evidence is mounting about the dark side of technology). He calls the constellation of dangers "iDisorder." Full book title is *iDisorder: Understanding Our Obsession with Technology and Overcoming Its Hold on Us*.[30]

Rosen amasses page after page of evidence that technology increasingly controls our lives in dysfunctional and pervasive ways, from the mildly rude checking-out of text messages every few minutes regardless of who we are with, to the more psychotic descent into schizoid behaviors of delusions, hallucinations, and social avoidance.

Rosen takes the reader through a range of debilitating problems that technology does not cause but that it naturally enables. He outlines the evidence on the following domains of distortion associated with the increased presence of digital technology in our lives: narcissism (it's all about me, me, me), obsession (checking in with our technology 24/7), addiction (wallowing in impulsivity, sensation seeking, and social deviance), bipolarity (feeling high or low depending on one's social-networking digital day), ADHD (being jerked around by the instant gratification of hyperlinks with accompanying information overload, poor sleep, and an inability to stay with and complete tasks), decrease in quality relationships (including lower empathy), hypochondria (a little medical knowledge is a dangerous thing), fixation on appearance (associated with eating disorders), schizoid behavior (becoming more solitary, emotionally cold, and detached), and voyeurism (watching rather than engaging in). Whew! That can fill your day!

Rosen has been at this for a while, beginning his scientific studies in the 1980s and continuing to the present. He concludes that we have an increasing dependency on technology, but the worse part is that we are "happily traipsing down a road to an iDisorder," unaware of what is happening to us.[31]

Rosen's main argument, as is the theme of this chapter, is not that we should discount technology; rather, it is that we need to be aware of its dangerous downside in order to reduce its addictive power and maximize its prodigious upside. The basic question is, who is in charge here—human or machine?

When it comes to education and schooling, a whole new set of issues become evident. School boredom has no chance against the addictive digital draw of the outside world. Within schools, technology is conspicuous by its absence or by its superficial, ad hoc use. *Stratosphere* wants to change that. How can technology help us by opening up the world to deeply engaged learning and worldwide, collaborative problem-solving? In a word, technology, well used, can help us race rapidly to a future that humankind wants and will find fulfilling.

The rest of this book makes the case that (a) schools in the United States are in a crisis, (b) ham-handed solutions over the past 30 years have made matters worse, and (c) certain developments have occurred

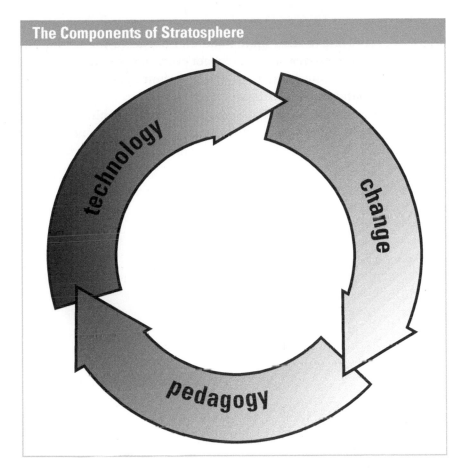

The Components of Stratosphere

technology

change

pedagogy

Exhibit 2.1

in both pedagogy and technology (up to this point independently) that make the identification of a powerful solution decidedly possible in the very near future. In essence, the solution consists of the integration of advances in pedagogy (especially built on how we learn), in technology (especially around engagement), and in change knowledge (especially around making change easier). If we get the combination right, the floodgates of learning will open and there will be an unstoppable explosion of energy and participation by all that will benefit individuals and the world alike.

In Chapter 3 I begin with pedagogy and change, concluding with an image of the new pedagogy and why the prospects for change may be better than we think. Chapter 4 takes a direct look at the digital drivers—disappointing so far, but containing dreamy possibilities—that consist of radically new pedagogy that turns the classroom and school on their heads, something possible only with a new and prominent role for technology. Chapter 5 takes up the question of design for change and change knowledge—what we know about achieving change on a large scale. What will it take to get what we call "whole-system reform"—all schools, all districts, all states/provinces, all countries, all students, and all teachers? Exciting new design criteria, embedded within our whole-system change knowledge, make for great possibilities in the near future. Finally, in Chapter 6 we try to make peace with technology. As sinister as technology can become, it has far more upside than downside potential. It is time to define the learning game as racing *with* technology.

Welcome to the stratosphere.

Pedagogy and Change: Essence as Easy

It has been said that Asian students do so well wherever they are because they are industrious while U.S. students are lazy. I don't know about you, but I get lazy too when I am bored. There is only one thing worse than being bored and that is being responsible for teaching the bored under conditions that restrict what you can do. *Stratosphere* will make the lives of both students and teachers exciting. Their learning fates are intimately conjoined. In this chapter I focus on "change as easy" for students and for adults, and on the new pedagogy, which dovetails with change as easy (the hard part will be changing the institutions that support the old way—but that's not as hard as one might surmise).

I am a great fan of what we call "the skinny."[1] What is the essence of a problem and its solution? Almost all great breakthroughs come from focusing, working on a small number of ambitious goals, and creating something different and elegant in simplicity. In skinny solutions the design work is hard, but the use is engaging and even hard work seems easy. What the skinny will have to capture in education is two big things: *engagement* and *efficiency* (high yield). The potential integration of technology, pedagogy, and change knowledge can be designed to create learning experiences that operate to produce high, natural yields in what is learned.

Our colleague Phil Schlechty has spent most of the past 40 years trying to convince educators that it is not the performance of teachers that counts but rather the performance of students.[2] Learning is all about purposeful *engagement*. The engaged student is attentive, committed, persistent, and finds meaning and value in the tasks, says Schlechty. The engaged student finds that learning is worth the effort (high yield).

Leaving technology aside for the moment, let's consider how change might occur for the student and for the adult (the teacher). It turns out that recent research shows that such change may be easier than we thought.

Change and the Student

In Ontario from 2003 to 2014 we increased high-school graduation from 68 percent to 84 percent across the 900 schools. And it was fairly easy to do! I will tell you why and how later in this section, but first let's go to some revealing recent research. David Yeager and Gregory Walton wrote a review of research, "Social-Psychological Interventions in Education: They're Not Magic."[3] They found that short exercises that focus on students' thoughts, feelings, and beliefs in and about school can lead to large gains in student achievement as well as reduce achievement gaps months and even years later. Targeting students' subjective experiences is the key. Engagement via meaning is the route. This is the skinny on effective learning interventions.

The authors provide numerous examples, two of which I cite here. One study found that students who attended an eight-session workshop teaching them that their brain is a muscle and grows with effort achieved a dramatic increase in math achievement over the remainder of the school year, while a control group that received workshops on study skills showed no gains. Another study found that when students were asked to write about core personal values in a 15- to 20-minute writing exercise, the gap between African American and European American students shrank by almost 40 percent by the end of the semester. The gain was maintained through the use of additional writing interventions.

How could a brief psychological exercise have such an impact on what are usually deemed insurmountable problems? The short answer is that it taps into student mindsets in a way that opens up subtle new ways of relating to learning opportunities. What looks like a small intervention can appear quite large to a student. Interventions do not have to remain in the conscious mind for them to have an impact. If a message affects how a student thinks and feels about school or about self, it can work away in the subconscious mind. Yeager and Walton call these "stealthy" interventions—a quality that increases their effectiveness. None of the interventions tried to directly persuade students to think differently: "rather than simply delivering an appeal to a student who passively receives it, each intervention enlisted students as actively [and unknowingly] participating in or generating the intervention itself."[4]

These "stealthy" interventions have the added benefit that they do not stigmatize students. They do not single them out for needing help. Stealthy interventions are brief and thus much less expensive. They can be long lasting, say Yeager and Walton, because they set in motion social, psychological, and intellectual processes that result in initial success, greater sense of belongingness, and a belief that students can learn more than they thought possible. Interventions like these, with corresponding supports, can alter students' academic trajectories.

Yeager and Walton do not assume that it is simply a matter of going to scale with these types of interventions. The interventions require on the part of educators *theoretical expertise* (understanding the psychological experiences at play) and *contextual expertise* (understanding the background and experiences of students in the local context). The skinny, in other words, demands sophistication of design and good teachers in order to get ease of use (see Chapter 5).

At the beginning of this section I mentioned that increasing high school graduation in Ontario's 900 secondary schools was easier than expected. It involves knowing where every student stands, intervening in a non-judgmental manner, providing a good program mix, improving teaching and learning, and connecting schools deeply to their community.

Here is how Ontario did it. The Ministry of Education instituted a Student Success Strategy, which focused on two core facets: increase the number of course options available to students inside and outside of the classroom and provide one-on-one support to students who need extra help and encouragement to complete their courses. This information is fully documented on their website.[5]

In the first instance, the Ministry of Education put into place a number of initiatives:

- Allow for specialist high skills majors where students can start to build experiences that lead to a specific career through select courses, workplace experience, and certification

- Enable students to count cooperative learning experience toward two compulsory credits

- Expand elearning initiatives

- Institute dual credits—a student can apply the credit to their high school diploma as well as to a college certificate or diploma program or an apprenticeship
- Provide additional teacher resources and professional learning focusing on math and literacy
- Adopt credit rescue and recovery programs
- Develop more structured alternative learning programs
- Build leadership capacity in schools, focusing on increased student achievement

In the second instance, the ministry developed Student Success Teams.[6] These teams comprised core members, including the school principal, a Student Success teacher, a special education teacher, and a guidance counsellor. These teams worked to help personalize school for students who were struggling, regardless of the reason for their difficulty. Much of the work was akin to Yeager and Walton's social-psychological interventions focused on the subjective experiences of students. Students who worked with these teams received needed time and attention to help them achieve and guidance from the members to tap into additional supports (e.g., credit rescue) that would motivate them to continue. In this way, the two facets of the initiative worked in tandem.

In addition to the work in high schools, the ministry developed an initiative to gauge and increase student engagement at the Grades 7 to 12 levels. Each year, approximately 60 students from across the province serve as members of the Minister's Student Advisory Council. The goal of the council is to give a voice to students via their representatives, and through their efforts, increase school engagement for all students, including those at risk of dropping out.

In sum, we are getting some new consistency. We need to shift our approach to focus on the subjective experiences of students and engage them in new meaningful and exciting ways. Once we change our stance and approach education differently, it may take only small interventions to unleash major new learning trajectories. Change and learning, in other words, become immensely more productive, easier, and comparatively inexpensive.

Notice in this section that with the exception of additional elearning offerings by the Ontario Ministry of Education, the initiatives have capitalized on the human element of collaboration. Imagine what technology could do if used in the service of multiple stealthy learning interventions. If we get the pedagogy right and incorporate technology accordingly, learning will become easier, deeper, and more engaging. Students and teachers will be putting in long hours, but what they do won't feel like work. What we have seen in this section with students is only a particular instance of how humans learn. This means we should look for the same "essence as easy" when it comes to adults learning. The solution for teachers and the solution for students must come as a package.

Change and the Adult

In *The Progress Principle,* Teresa Amabile and Steven Kramer write about "using small wins to ignite joy, engagement and creativity at work."[7] It is the same concept we have just seen with students. Their research shows that the secret to better change "is creating the conditions for a great *inner work life*—the conditions that foster positive emotions, strong internal motivation, and favorable perceptions of colleagues and the work itself."[8] In studying various teams Amabile and Kramer found that even small events trigger big reactions. Making even small progress in meaningful work is the most powerful stimulant to wanting to do more.

Amabile and Kramer collected examples from workers of what seemed to be minor workday events that powerfully elevated or dampened feelings, thoughts, and motivation. What they found was that on days where people reported progress, they were more intrinsically motivated by the enjoyment and the challenges in the work. On setback days these same people were not only less intrinsically motivated, they were also less extrinsically motivated by recognition. Setbacks make people more generally apathetic to the work.

The researchers also created a measure of overall mood for the day. When they correlated this scale to progress and setbacks, they found that 76 percent of the best days were associated with progress and 67 percent of the worst days were connected to setbacks. Remember that the events affecting one's mood for the entire day or more are small—receiving kindness from someone else, solving a niggling problem, seeing something work for the first time. It is not extrinsic incentives, recognition, or even positive feedback that matters the most but rather progress in the work and managers who create the conditions that make progress more likely.

Once again the skinny: What matters most is progress in the work itself and paying attention to small wins and setbacks on a daily basis—this is the essence of change management. If people are involved in meaningful work, *and* if they feel capable, *and* if they are helped to make even small progress, they become more motivated and ready for the next challenges. Effective organizations foster conditions for these *positive progress loops* to prevail.

Of course, there is more to organizational effectiveness than small wins. Amabile and Kramer identify several catalytic factors (such as time, resources, autonomy, and help), and nourishment factors (respect, affiliation, and emotional support); however, that need not concern us here. The main point is that people—students and teachers alike, for example—need to feel and experience some regular progress. As the authors note, any video game designer knows that small steps of progress are essential for drawing players in.

Apparently, managers take these small things for granted while they focus on the bigger matters of plans, clear goals, data, allocation of resources, periodic recognition and rewards, and so on. Amabile and Kramer tested this hypothesis in one survey in which they asked 669 managers to rank five factors that could influence the motivation. One of the factors, "support for making progress in the work," came in last behind the other four: recognition, incentives, interpersonal support, and clear goals.[9] Similarly, in a convention of business executives from large companies, Amabile and Kramer asked the leaders what managers can do to motivate employees. They got the usual list with no mention of facilitating daily progress in work. When pressed, these leaders said, of course daily progress is motivating, but evidently they didn't think it was necessary to attend to it every day.

We will see later with students that the new pedagogy–technology combinations tap into, stimulate, and even create purpose and passion in what students want to learn. Amabile and Kramer essentially say that *adults*—teachers, in this case—must have the same motivational experiences. The magic of *Stratosphere* is that students and teachers are conjointly stimulated to engage in the pursuit of deeper learning: it is fueled by their passions and purposes. Both students and their teachers are turned on.

The New Pedagogy

How students best learn is becoming increasingly clear. It very much has to do with tapping into and leveraging their subjective selves. *Constructivism* as it has been called has been around a long time, but until recently it stayed mostly at the theoretical or minor levels. Now we see it more concretely, albeit still on a small scale. The new examples meet our criteria: being engaging and offering ease of use. By *ease of use*, I do not mean simple, but rather use as relatively easy because of the draw of engagement and the work with others (much how you find work when you are doing what you like). Let's look more closely.

Tony Wagner's *Creating Innovators* is a perfect example of the new pedagogy. He finds that innovative learners display curiosity, collaboration, and a desire to experiment and learn from such experiences. On our ease of use dimension, he draws on the work of Teresa Amabile, introduced earlier in this chapter. He adapts her creativity model which is based on three components: expertise (knowledge), creative thinking (problem solving), and motivation (intrinsic drive). Wagner considers motivation as the source of all good learning and unpacks it by concluding that intrinsic motivation is fueled by play (experimenting), purpose (wanting to make a difference), and passion (devoting yourself to something you find deeply meaningful).

Wagner's book is full of named examples of students and their mentors whose learning lives exemplify the qualities just mentioned. Take Kirk Phelps, who was both a high-school and a college dropout. Phelps reflects on his learning journey: "What you study is not that important. Knowing how to find those things that you are interested in is way, way more important."[10] Along the way he discovered that he liked to work with others to make tangible things. One of his teacher mentors also captured the new pedagogy when he said, "empowerment means students can go out and apply what they've learned to the problems that they've never seen before with parts that they've never used before."[11]

Wagner furnishes several other examples by name in both the STEM (Science, Technology, Engineering, and Mathematics) and the social innovation domains. He cites Laura White's development at Tulane University in New Orleans. Tulane University, led by its president, Scott Cowen, developed a social innovation theme catalyzed by the Hurricane Katrina disaster. The overall theme, called "Tulane Empowers," has seven pillars: public education, community health, the next generation of engaged citizens and leaders, disaster response and resilience, physical revitalization of the city and cultural arts, the center for teaching and learning, and social innovation. In one project, for example, White was part of Citizen Circles, in which people come together to address a social problem and share what they learn in the process of making change.[12]

All of these experiences contrast with the fundamental basis of schools as they are today. As Wagner says, schools currently reward individual competition, are subject based (versus problem based), and rely on extrinsic motivation (such as grades). By contrast in all of the successful examples, the students in question talk of doing things that are meaningful in the world, projects that focus on solving a problem, engaging in teamwork, and operating under conditions that encourage risk-taking. The new pedagogy involves helping students find purpose, passion, and experimental doing in a domain that stokes their desire to learn and keep on learning.

"Increasingly in the 21st century," argues Wagner, "what you know is far less important than what you can do with what you know. The interest in and ability to create new knowledge to solve new problems is the single most important skill that all students must master today. All successful innovators have mastered the ability to learn on their own 'in the moment' and then apply that knowledge in new ways."[13] The new pedagogy that Wagner documents does not involve a long list: its emphasis is on addressing real problems, intellectual risk-taking and trial-and-error problem solving, collaboration in learning, and intrinsic motivation.

This is the same theme that Sir Ken Robinson has been so elegantly articulating in the last decade and more. No matter how clear he has been, people still think of him as a spokesman for the arts. He does like the arts, but fundamentally he is an advocate for creativity for every child whether it is drama, science, math, or history. For Robinson *the element* consists of "aptitude and passion" that come alive under the conditions of "attitude and opportunity." He gives scores of case examples of students who were not good at or otherwise not enjoying traditional schooling whose creative energies were unleashed in a torrent of learning when they discovered or were helped to find their passion and purpose—just like Wagner's "creative collaborators." Being creative in one's area of interest is for everyone, says Robinson. Although he doesn't delve far into it, Robinson makes the point that "digital technologies are now putting in the hands of millions of people everywhere, unprecedented tools for creativity in sound, in design, in sciences and in the arts."[14] According to Robinson, everyone has creative potential, we can all learn to be more creative, and "creativity loves collaboration and creativity thrives on diversity"—another statement confirming the new pedagogy for schools. Furthermore, it is never too late for learning. Some people are late bloomers or never had a chance to find their interests at an earlier age. Robinson doesn't want to make room for the arts in the curriculum; he wants to make room *for the students*.

Teachers are needed, but it is a new role that is required—the teacher as change agent. Robinson calls them mentors who play four roles: recognizing, encouraging, facilitating, and stretching. Current schooling does not measure up to these possibilities, and the proportion of *misfits* (those not served well by traditional schooling) is growing larger with technology ironically playing a supporting role (it is more interesting than school). Most current students, traditional or not, do not find school engaging. Nor do their teachers, I would venture to say. This is why something has to give. While the change is radical it will not be as hard as it may seem if we can organize technology, the new pedagogy, and change knowledge to guide the transformation.

Marc Prensky goes down the same path. He makes the case that current reformers are busy trying to establish better versions of what was needed for the 20th century instead of creating and implementing a better, more future-oriented education for all of our kids. He calls for a solution that is deeply compatible with Wagner's and with our stratospheric integration of technology, pedagogy, and change knowledge. The answer, Prensky says, is to base the new education on a clear proven pedagogy that he calls "partnering with our students":

> "Partnering" is a catchall term for approaches that include problem-based learning, case-based learning, inquiry-based learning, student-centered learning, and others… At their core, they are all variations on the same central pedagogical idea…*an end to teaching by "telling," and a reassignment of roles for the teacher and students.*[15]

Prensky also finds, as did Wagner, that collaboration or peer-to-peer learning (designed by a change agent teacher) is an enormous "free resource" dramatically aided by technology. When he refers to partners in learning, Prensky means *both* players. We need to inspire teachers as well as students. Unleashing the creative energy of both is essential for any solution to have depth and longevity.

We get more support for these new directions of learning and living from author Jonah Lehrer in his book *Imagine: How Creativity Works.* Lehrer defines creativity as "the ability to imagine what has never existed."[16] He offers two critical insights. One is that cognition and imagination are related intimately but not in a step-by-step fashion. He suggests that people gain new ideas when they work on problems rationally, get frustrated, and then when on a break from direct problem-solving, discover new solutions—the well-known I-get-my-best-ideas-in-the-shower phenomenon. His second insight, fundamentally compatible with stratosphere, is that everyone can become creative under the right learning conditions.

The first idea—that insight occurs when we balance direct engagement in a task with a kind of detached insouciance—is confirmed in new research on the brain's activity centers. As Lehrer describes, the left hemisphere of the brain tries to seek answers in the obvious places (recall McGilchrist from Chapter 1), but sooner than later tires of the problem if it is at all difficult. When one gets away from direct immersion in a problem, the right hemisphere can still be, so to speak, working on the problem in subconscious ways. At some point, and in ways that are not easily traceable, the "answer" seems to come out of the blue and in a surprisingly complete form.

Using advanced techniques of fMRI brain scanning, Lehrer reports that scientists have found that the suddenness of the insight is preceded by equally sudden bursts of brain activity: "Thirty milliseconds before the answer erupts into consciousness, there's a spike of gamma-wave rhythm, which is the highest electrical frequency generated by the brain."[17]

In other words, tackling and staying with problems may not be the best way of solving them. To achieve a breakthrough, it may be necessary to get away from the clenched constraints of left-brain literalism. This insight gives a whole new meaning to "thinking outside the box." Best thinking is outside one box but still inside one's head in another box.

Lehrer spends the first half of his book describing examples of new insights of people working alone. The learning rule is this: work on a problem directly, but build in times to get away for reflection or immersion in something else. As Lehrer puts it, "Are you stuck on a challenge that seems impossible? Lie down on a couch by a sunny window."[18] Lehrer's evidence shows that "the essential element is a steady stream of alpha waves emanating from the right hemisphere" that are associated with relaxing activities in which you get away from the direct problem.[19] This flow occurs when we are in a relaxed state of mind because "we are more likely to direct the spotlight of attention *inward* toward that stream of remote associations emanating from the right hemisphere."[20] When attention is directed outward to the details of the problem (or distracted by external hyper-stimuli), we miss the connections that lead to insights.

This approach can sound like voodoo learning, but let's consider complementary practical implications. First, the advice is that when we are stuck, we need to get away from the complex problem at hand—meditate, do something else, relax. This advice is practical because it is not difficult to follow and often yields surprising results. On the other side, we can immediately see that excessive bombardment by outside forces distracts us in the wrong way—we need, instead, pockets of downtime.

Just as periods of solitude are crucial to learning, Lehrer also shows how the group is essential for the solving of complex problems. This idea, too, is complicated because it does not hold true for the extremes in group relationships. Either too much sameness or too much scatter is problematic—the extremes are equally problematic. Interacting only with the like-minded or of being hyperlinked to scads of strangers is dysfunctional. Creative collaboration has a sweet spot that consists of the right mixture of established relationships and newcomers.

Lehrer cites the research of Brian Uzzi, who studied the success of Broadway musicals from 1877 to 1990. Uzzi measured a concept he labeled as Q, the degree of social intimacy of the people creating the production. When the Q score was low (having limited group closeness) or when the Q score was high (collaborating only with friends), commercial and critical success of the musical was low. Broadway musicals that showed evidence of "intermediate levels of social intimacy" were 2.5 times more likely to be winners.[21] The mixture of friends and newcomers allowed a degree of comfort along with access to new ideas.

Lehrer also sheds new light on why brainstorming fails. Brainstorming is ineffective because, by definition (norms of non-judgment), there is no critical feedback. Brainstorming groups think of far fewer ideas than if the same number of people worked alone and then pooled their ideas, especially if the pooling encouraged constructive criticism of each other's ideas. As we will see in Chapter 4, feedback to students during learning is probably the most powerful teaching strategy we can use. Learning from mistakes is the key.

The implications of Lehrer's work on creativity take us right back to Wagner, Robinson, and Prensky. Consider a survey that Lehrer cites. When teachers were asked whether they wanted creative kids in their classroom, every teacher said yes. But when teachers were asked to rate their favorite students, their answers gave another story: "Judgments for the favorite student were negatively correlated with creativity; judgments for the least favorite student were positively correlated with creativity."[22]

The creative students were harder to teach (under today's pedagogical conditions). What is missing for most students is the new pedagogy that would enable them to find and pursue their passion, purpose, and play (as Wagner put it), work with a team to study, understand, and help address real-life problems, and develop their talent through perseverance and constructive feedback.

Most important, Lehrer has reinforced the point that creativity can be designed for and fostered in every student—not just so there can be more fulfilled individuals, but also because the mobilization of individual and collective talent is essential for global survival. This different approach to learning could bring a marked increase in the level of innovation, entrepreneurship, problem solving, empathy, teamwork, and sustainability. It is the future.

A new book by Daniel Goleman and colleagues furnishes more ideas and evidence that allow us to feel hopeful about the trends we are discussing. Keep in mind though that these new directions must be *integrated* into a comprehensive plan, not treated as add-ons. First, the good news. The book, *Ecoliterate: How Educators Are Cultivating Emotional, Social, and Ecological Intelligence,* documents many examples of practice in schools and communities that reflect exciting new learning in which teachers and students are pursuing and fanning the flames of purpose, passion, and ecological sustainability.[23]

The authors focus on examples of projects in ecological improvement pertaining to coal, oil, water, and food. They establish five pillars: (1) developing empathy for all forms of life; (2) embracing sustainability as a community practice; (3) making the invisible visible; (4) anticipating unintended consequences; and (5) understanding how nature sustains life.

What they have created represents a fine curriculum, but we must understand how it fits with the new pedagogy. Ecological and human sustainability should be seamless. The right brain will tell us that ecological concerns and human life are not separable. Furthermore, we won't get anywhere if the ecological agenda is seen as adding to the curriculum. Given that one of our criteria for maximizing learning is "steeped in real-life problem solving" (see Chapter 4), the entire curriculum needs to be redefined: the whole raison d'être of schooling becomes a single expanded entity called "learning about and for life," and doing it in a passionate and purposeful manner. We are talking about a total makeover—made practical by the integrated forces of technology, pedagogy, and change knowledge.

The themes of the new pedagogy will appear throughout this book, but this chapter is on essence as easy. How easy will it be to create this new system? Well, for starters, it will be far easier than trying to hold the current deeply dysfunctional system together. The move to the new system will not be simple, but it won't be as daunting as it appears. On the admittedly difficult side, it has all the characteristics of what Clayton Christensen and Michael Raynor called "a disruptive innovation."[24]

Christensen and Raynor said that current practice persists because the system keeps trying to improve the existing product (they call this phenomenon "sustaining innovations"). Disruptive technologies are *initially inferior* to existing practice. They are inferior because they have not yet had time to develop, and it takes a bunch of users to develop products on the ground. For this reason the disruptive innovation has a hard time catching on; however, *this is only temporary until the new improvement cycle accelerates. Stratosphere* tells us that we are at the beginning of what will turn out to be a rapidly improving learning cycle.

How bad is schooling at present? I won't marshal the reams of evidence available on the topic, but one dramatic graph sent to me by Lee Jenkins will make the point in an instant. Jenkins asked more than 2,000 teachers what grade they teach and what percentage of their students love school. We can predict the results, but they are nonetheless shocking (Exhibit 3.1). Ninety-five percent of students love school in Kindergarten, but by Grade 9, the feeling has steadily declined to 37 percent; a slight incline occurs in the final grades of high school (with the select group of students who remain). This graph, based on estimates from the teachers, represents a hell of a lot of disengaged students. If you asked students directly, you would find these figures equally problematic or worse. In its report *My Voice,* the Quaglia Institute found

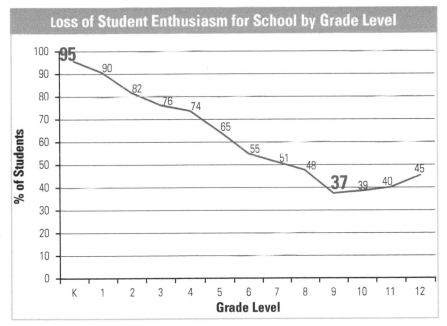

Exhibit 3.1

that student–teacher relationships weakened as students went from elementary to middle to high school.[25] For those students who have a bent for innovation, such as those Wagner, Prensky, and others describe, boredom in regular classes is sky-high. Even with the best teachers, says Prensky, kids "still say with consistency they're bored 50–70 percent of the time."[26] The sad thing is that most students don't know what they are missing.

On top of this, and more than incidentally, the lot of teachers is not much better. The 2011 *MetLife Survey of the American Teacher* shows a sharp decline in teacher satisfaction and engagement. In a remarkably short time—two years—teacher satisfaction decreased by 15 points (from 59 percent to 44 percent). Almost one in three teachers (29 percent) say that they would like to leave teaching in the near future, compared to one in four (17 percent) two years earlier.[27] These numbers are bad enough in absolute terms, but downright alarming when you consider the trend.

The solution in stratosphere counteracts these dismal realities by creating conditions for deep engagement of both students and teachers. In some ways teachers are more important than students because each teacher affects, for better or worse, between 25 and 150 students per day. Students will not have a good day at school when every second teacher is frustrated and every third teacher would rather be somewhere else.

Conclusion

Is it possible to be optimistic given the miasmic alienation and boredom of the majority of students and their teachers I just portrayed? I believe so. Aside from the obvious reason that the status quo is experiencing intolerable, ever-worsening stress, the constellation of forces in stratosphere that I identify can form a practical basis for building a better future. These forces are so powerful and so connective that it is almost inevitable that we will see creative breakthroughs in the near future.

This future reality will have to be pushed and pulled, but may happen in the same way that creative solutions pop up after we have exhausted direct remedies. The encouraging news is that the disruptive innovations and corresponding improvement cycles of Christensen and Raynor are already under way (these developments are the subject of Chapter 4).

I am optimistic and think this is a case of essence as easy for four main reasons in combination:

1. The old technology of tell and test or experience and evoke does not work, and it is becoming clearer to more people that it can never work.

2. Examples of the new pedagogy of partnering with students are rapidly under development. These examples will only advance in quality and availability all the more so because technology can be the great accelerator. Indeed, this is what the stratosphere phenomenon predicts.

3. There will be a great appetite for the new way. Passion, purpose, and the new pedagogy are natural winners because they tap into and activate what is human—doing something intrinsically meaningful and of value to oneself, one's peers, and the world at large. You don't get any closer to secular spiritualism than this.

4. It really is easier than we might think for the simple reasons that people will be doing what they like, and many people will be helping. Many hands and minds do make light work.

We have already seen in the first half of this chapter that a little connection can go a long way. Prensky takes up the same theme in talking about easy-to-do, big impact steps. As he puts it, "if, tomorrow, every teacher in America spent 20 minutes of class time asking each student what her or his passion was, and then later used that information to understand each student more deeply and differentiate their instruction accordingly, education would take giant positive steps forward overnight."[28] Prensky has 10 other measures that take minimal effort on the part of teachers, but have great potential positive impact on children's education:

1. Doing less "telling" while allowing students to research the answers to guiding questions on their own

2. Always connecting what is taught with real-world outcomes

3. Helping students distinguish the unchanging "verbs" (skills) of education from the rapidly changing "nouns" (tools)

4. Treating students as learning partners

5. Employing students' own tools (particularly video and cellphones) for learning

6. Using more peer-to-peer teaching

7. Offering students far more choices, rather than mandating what all must read or do

8. Allowing students to be the primary users (and maintainers) of classroom technology

9. Sharing success via short videos posted on sites such as YouTube or TeacherTube

10. Regularly connecting students with the world via free, secure tools such as Skype and ePals[29]

In summary, we are at the beginning of a powerful disruptive innovation that will grow in leaps and bounds. We must have our wits about us to take advantage of this once-in-a-century opportunity. We must take a trial-experiment-learn-refine approach to this next phase. We must, in other words, take a learning approach. The new journey will be bumpy, but less bumpy than what we are going through now. And it will be relatively easy with bursts of progress.

Let's also be clear that the education revolution that Wagner, Robinson, Lehrer, and others are calling for is to create a system where every student finds his or her particular purpose and passion—what Robinson calls "the element." We have always known that purpose and passion are at the core of star business entrepreneurs and athletes. The difference in stratosphere is that *every* student is enabled to find his or her element.

Technology, especially as it is now becoming, will be a great partner in this profound learning enterprise. But equally we need the new pedagogy to be a dynamic partner. We need learners proactively in charge of their own learning-how-to-learn. And for the latter we need teachers and other mentors who can design and oversee the learning process. The remaining chapters are about these matters. Technology will loom increasingly large as a player. If we get this right, ultimately what we want and what technology wants in education will be the same thing.

Digital Disappointments and Dreams

The integration of technology and pedagogy to maximize learning must meet four criteria (Exhibit 4.1). It must be irresistibly engaging; elegantly efficient (challenging but easy to use); technologically ubiquitous; and steeped in real-life problem solving.

Exhibit 4.1 Criteria for Integrating Technology and Pedagogy	
1.	Irresistibly engaging
2.	Elegantly efficient
3.	Technologically ubiquitous
4.	Steeped in real-life problem solving

Irresistibly engaging is what it means to be rapt, or in a state of "flow" where time has no meaning. Our stratosphere innovations must have this quality. Second, these new products must be elegantly easy to use—simple to get hooked on and natural to use—challenging yes, but because we are drawn in not so daunting. A crucial point in these developments is that as innovations they do not further complicate the lives of students and teachers, but, on the contrary, they make their learning *easier and more interesting.* Rarely do we experience changes that give us a net advantage from the beginning.

Third, the first two criteria cannot be met unless technology is at our disposal 24/7. Finally, these experiences must be steeped in real-life problem-solving projects—learning that creates the conditions for individual and group success on a global scale. It is important to note that when problem-solving projects permeate the curriculum, we will be teaching *entrepreneurialism*. Innovative analysis and insights, whether applied to STEM problems or social innovations, cultivate the habits of entrepreneurs—another key learning goal for the 21st century.

As exciting as these criteria are, they have yet to be applied. No program or system in the world currently meets these criteria. I consider the current state of play under the headings "Digital Disappointments" and "Digital Dreaming."

As one example, let us consider the current reform movement in the United States in terms of three pillars of the educated student: standards, assessment, and instruction or pedagogy (Exhibit 4.2). Currently priorities are being placed on standards and assessment while the solution in stratosphere must be driven by pedagogy. The big breakthroughs that I describe in this book are all driven by deeper conceptions of learning. Fortunately, they can be incredibly accelerated by innovations in

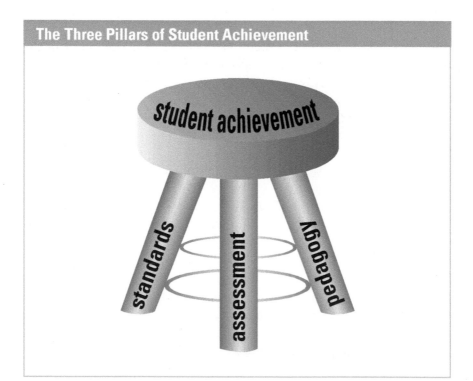

The Three Pillars of Student Achievement

student achievement

standards   assessment   pedagogy

Exhibit 4.2

technology—as long as *we get the causal sequence right:* pedagogy to technology and then back and forth, back and forth. If there is any racing to the top it is humankind *with* machines. Yes, when you are in a fast machine it sometimes controls you, but ultimately the machine is there to serve you—to do things that you could never do without it.

Digital Disappointments

Strictly speaking I am not going to take up simply *digital* disappointments. As we will see they are just as much a problem of poor conceptualization as they are of technology. But they are ultimately digital failures because progress requires that good ideas become hitched to technology. There is no way to accomplish the ideas without the power of machines.

The biggest culprit is 21st century skills that seem to have been around since at least 1990. To state the conclusion up front: The skills as treated are too vague to be of any use, and they almost always leave out pedagogy (learning experiences for getting there). Typical is Bernie Trilling and Charles Fadel's *21st Century Skills: Learning for Life in Our Times.*[1] Their 21st century knowledge and skills rainbow consists of three sets of skills that have numerous subsets of skills. The three categories are learning and innovation skills; information, media, and technology skills; and life and career skills. The subsets include critical thinking, communication, creativity (for learning and innovation); information literacy, media literacy, and information and communication technology (for technology skills); and flexibility, initiative, social and cross-cultural interaction, productivity and accountability, and leadership and responsibility (for life and career skills). And each of these has numerous subdivided skills.

Trilling and Fadel offer a support system infrastructure that includes standards, assessment, curriculum and instruction, professional development, and learning environments. At this level it is good stuff, but trying to implement it may well lead to disappointment. Oddly enough there is not much about technology as fundamental to the solution except for the odd example of individual schools (such as teams of elementary students in the Netherlands creating landscape designs for the front of their school). Good to do, but it doesn't add up.

Countless school districts, provinces, states, and countries have embraced the 21st century skills mantra. The Government of Alberta's

Inspiring Action on Education is an example.[2] Alberta's rainbow of 21st century learning skills includes seven skills sets: critical thinking and problem solving; creativity and innovation; social responsibility and global awareness; communication; digital literacy; lifelong learning, self-direction, and personal management; and collaboration and leadership. It turns out that inspiration is not much of a basis for action. In our change work we have found that considered action results in inspiration more than the other way around. Alberta is an example. To date, it has obtained more mileage from the Alberta Initiative for School Improvement that seeds innovative ideas coming from districts than it has from highlighting its 21st century learning skills.

Nancy Watson and I conducted an assessment of progress in 21st century learner skills for the Stupski Foundation of California.[3] We included the much-publicized Cisco-Intel-Microsoft multi-year international project, Assessment & Teaching of 21st Century Skills (ATC21S). The project includes a familiar list of competencies under three categories: ways of thinking (creativity; critical thinking; problem solving; decision making); ways of working (communication; collaboration); and tools for working (information literacy and ICT, or Information and Communication Technology). It also includes skills for living in the world (citizenship, life and career, and personal and social responsibility).[4]

We examined briefly five other examples as well: the Partnership for Next Generation Learning in the United States; the Waters Foundation work on systems thinking in Tucson; and three top-performing entities in the world: Ontario, Finland, and Singapore. We were not being overly critical when we gave our Stupski report the title *The Slow Road to Higher Order Skills*.

No matter how you cut it, we are not making progress on this agenda. By and large the goals are too vague, having a glitzy attraction. When we start down the pathway of specificity, the focus is on standards and assessment (which does help with clarity), but the crucial third pillar—pedagogy, or fostering actual learning—is neglected. And aside from its use in assessment schemes, which is a contribution, technology plays little role in *learning*, surely the main point of all this highfalutin fanfare.

When we consider technology and schooling, we are in for much more digital disappointment. Despite the astounding and abounding creativity and ubiquity of technology in the world at large, it is barely showing up in schools. The Nellie Mae Education Foundation commissioned a report, *Integrating Technology with Student-Centered Learning*.[5]

Here is what the report found:

- Only 8 percent of teachers fully integrate technology into the classroom.

- Some 43 percent of students feel unprepared to use technology as they look to higher education or their work life (and I would venture to say that many of those who feel prepared got that way from their outside-the-school digital learning).

- Only 23 percent of teachers feel that they could integrate technology in the classroom.

- The organizational support for the use of technology in schools is badly underdeveloped (availability of digital media, shared vision, school culture, technical support, leadership and the school, district and state levels, assessment systems, and so on).

What is additionally worrying is that even when technology is the center of attention, good pedagogy goes missing. The Media Awareness Network in Canada is tracking the evolution of young Canadians in a wired world. In one study the Network selected a sample of 10 teachers who were known as being successful in creating excellent learning environments for their students (one elementary and one high-school teacher in each of five regions: the North, the West, Ontario, Quebec, and the Atlantic). In other words, the sample was selected to get at the most advanced learning environments. All teachers surveyed indicated that their students "loved working and playing with smartphones, iPods, iPads, computers, and networked devices of all kinds." When the researchers examined uses more closely, they concluded that students were "not so savvy surfers": "In spite of the fact that young people demonstrate a facility with online tools, many students lack the skills they need to use those tools effectively for learning… There is also a real propensity on the part of students to take what they find online as given."[6]

In other words, making digital devices available and helping teachers and students use them is the easy part—but it isn't pedagogy. The *Young Canadians in a Wired World* report concluded that teachers are largely on their own when it comes to figuring out how to use technology to enhance learning. This is more disturbing than it seems because what looks like progress really isn't. In 2000, 44 percent of students in a Network survey reported that the internet was their preferred source of information; by 2005 the figure was well over 80 percent and now must be in the high 90s. The mere availability and even widespread use of technology of course is not the point. When the Media Awareness

Network did find effective use of integrating technology, it was "precisely because they [teachers] focused on pedagogy, were comfortable with not being the tech expert in the room, had strong classroom management skills, and saw online pitfalls as teachable moments."[7]

Even high performers in PISA (Programme for International Student Assessment), such as Finland, do not fare well when it comes to pedagogical use of technology. A team of researchers from the University of Jyväskylä is studying the implementation of 21st century skills teaching of the ATC21S in Finnish schools. So far they have found that while 21st century skills are contained in the core National Curriculum, "they do not usually show up in the classroom," and "technology is well available, but the pedagogically innovative or effective use of ICT is still very rare."[8] In other words, even in countries touted for their leadership in education, use of the new scenarios as discussed in this book is only sporadic.

We can up the ante and still find we have a long way to go. For example, as great as the Khan Academy is (and it is phenomenally great), it still requires a great teacher. Sal Khan was working as a hedge-fund manager when he began teaching his cousin in New Orleans basic math concepts by video from his New York location. He was so successful that he started to use YouTube, established the Khan Academy, and made some 3,000 videos available. Well over 130 million viewings of the lessons have occurred, and the number is growing rapidly. Anyone who has learned from these videos knows that they are fabulous instructional exemplars of clarity. For the purposes of stratosphere, Khan is an incredibly great 20th century pedagogue using 21st century technology (and not the most advanced at that). As Prensky says, all students should have a great explainer, someone they can watch over and over again until they get it. The videos, as Prensky tells, are *just explanations* (taken to a high point of clarity and ease of use). Khan has not invented a new way to teach math, but has improved the delivery system of the old way.[9]

Recall our discussion of disruptive innovations. Early examples are inferior but are the beginning of a new cycle of improvement. As Prensky puts it, there are "better ways for many of our dropouts and failing kids to learn; not just by hearing explanations and doing examples, but rather by doing real work in context, in fun and appropriate settings"[10]—aka the new pedagogy. Test results can increase relative to the old system, but applying knowledge is not advanced.

We get further evidence of the limited impact of technology on student achievement from the review of research that Michael Young and his colleagues did on "serious gaming for education."[11] They found some evidence of positive effects of video games on language learning, history, and physical education (because games could simulate useful learning conditions in these subjects); however, they found little support for positive impact in science and math.

The biggest problem, according to Young and his colleagues, is that "educational video games are most frequently researched as the primary means by which the player learns, removing the instructor and allowing the student to complete his or her learning in isolation."[12] In other words, these innovations (or at least the research on them) *omit the teacher*. It is as if pedagogy is irrelevant. The authors' obvious conclusion is that video games should be implemented "in concert with good teaching." Sound instructional design, skilled teaching, and quality implementation will be required. Most of all, partnership between teachers and students (and among teachers and students) will be essential.

In a recent survey by the Joan Ganz Cooney Center, researchers found that 50 percent of the teachers report using digital games in their classrooms at least twice a week.[13] Of course this is not quality implementation let alone integration with pedagogy, but it does show that there may be a growing awareness and appetite for stratospheric solutions with "essence as easy" being a very attractive proposition.

We can add to this mix the rapid expansion of online learning that, up to this point, is largely about access. The Evergreen Education Group is keeping tabs on these developments with its annual review.[14] At last tally the percentage of districts and states with online learning offerings has been increasing at an annual rate of 25 percent. Florida has almost 260,000 course enrolments in its Florida Virtual School. Since access is no longer an issue, one must consider pedagogy as well as the change plan for quality implementation.

In short, overall we find little evidence of the impact of technology on learning (at least not yet, which is my point). In one sense this finding is obvious. We used to call this "on the risk of appraising non-events." If the innovation has not been implemented, it can hardly have much impact. So, we need to place this finding in perspective: implemented examples of the new pedagogy are few, although we got a glimpse of it from Wagner and Prensky in the last chapter.

In the meantime, the best large-scale assessment of the impact of instructional practices on student learning comes from John Hattie's meta-assessment of more than 800 studies worldwide.[15] Hattie considered effect sizes of 0.40 and above as worthwhile. The big winners were reciprocal teaching, 0.74 (in which teachers interact with students to make the students' thinking and questions about learning more explicit);

feedback, 0.73; teaching students self-verbalization, 0.64; and meta-cognition strategies, 0.69. At the lower end, below the cut-off point, were simulations and gaming, 0.33; and web-based learning, 0.18. The point of course is not that technology is less effective, but that *it is being grossly underutilized pedagogically*.

Along the same vein, Bruce Dixon and Susan Einhorn state that students' right to learn is being denied across the world because of lack of access to learning experiences and technology that is not so expensive to make available. They talk about "the elusive 21st Century Skills of Self-Directedness and Collaboration" that are part of the new pedagogy.[16] They are not specific about how to get there. The latter, indeed, is the purpose of stratosphere.

In short, technology and schooling are operating at cross-purposes and have been doing so for some time. As long as digital immersion and schooling function in isolation, and are not steeped in real-life problem solving, we will not see any progress. Sophisticated goals require sophisticated technology. Fortunately the dreams are becoming more vivid.

Digital Dreaming

When Ontario Premier Dalton McGuinty (whom I work for) suggested in September 2010 that cellphones and tablets might have useful educational applications, he was savaged in the press. Turns out he was ahead of his time. In the January 2012 issue of the magazine *Toronto Life*, there is an article called "Gadget Goes to School."[17]

Figuring out how to live and learn with gadgets is still a conundrum. This is part of an early stage in a new, more radical improvement cycle. Amid the relentless proliferation of mobile devices (close the door—they are coming in the windows) is a new generation of teachers who are embracing the use of classroom technology. In May 2011 the mammoth Toronto District School Board (TDSB), with its more than 500 schools, voted to lift the cellphone ban that had been enacted in 2007. Peter Chang, the TDSB superintendent charged with implementing the new policy, is going slowly—each teacher, he says, is to decide what is best for his or her class. The magazine article reports that "teachers who are already experimenting with BYOD (Bring Your Own Device) speak ecstatically of students' reactions—how engaged and enthusiastic they are about learning."[18]

I said earlier that the problem with technology is twofold: the digital world of the student is largely outside schools, and it is essentially undisciplined—all over the multi-tasking map. The magazine article details how in the TDSB one high-school teacher, Cate Cuttle, allows students to use their smartphones and describes the results as "thrilling." Students buddy up with many partners to do research together. Says Cuttle: "I absolutely feel a responsibility to prepare them for technology in the real world." As to the inequity of access to smartphones (only three-quarters of her students have them), this problem must be addressed; however, it will likely be eliminated within five years as mobile instruments become cheaper and more available. By far the greater problem is the gross underutilization of mobile devices.

In an adjacent school board—York Region District School Board—with almost 200 schools, we have another spawning ground for the spread of educational technologies. As reported in the article, teacher Royan Lee tells his students that they can bring whatever hand-held gadget they own. If a student doesn't have a device Lee pulls one from a box of school-owned gear. Lee says he will figure out good and bad use as he goes.

My point is that the floodgates are opening. It is now a matter of figuring out how to organize the use of ever expanding technologies that rapidly outrace pedagogy. A certain amount of evolutionary experimentation will be necessary in the early stages as is the case with Royan Lee. *Stratosphere* is about accelerating this sorting process.

Resistance is futile. The December 10, 2011, issue of *The Economist* contains a 10-page special report on video games.[19] The magazine reports on a PricewaterhouseCoopers (PwC) study that the video-game market was worth $56 billion in 2010. That is twice the size of the music industry, and three-fifths the size of the film industry, including DVDs. PwC predicts that video games will remain the fastest-growing form of media, reaching at least $82 billion by 2015. My message is, pedagogues, get in there! (Many of the games are in business, the military, the health sector, but not in education.) My prediction is that education will first succumb—as it is now doing—and then become an omnivore of digital learning. Essence as easy will prevail. Disruptive innovations will eventually get the upper hand.

As *The Economist* observes, one of the biggest changes has been the rise of mobile phones and now tablets as gaming devices. There were more than 5 billion worldwide mobile-phone subscriptions in 2011. The best games have huge potential for education because they incorporate the very design elements that new pedagogical practices emulate. By turning learning into a game, we create the intuitive interface with mobile devices (sophisticated design, elegant ease of use); we can create something that game designers call "juiciness" (lots of feedback).

"Gamefiers," or people who revel in developing games, says *The Economist*, make players want to perform difficult tasks and pay for the privilege. They "capture that sense of engagement by providing rapid, continuous feedback, a clear sense of progression and goals that are challenging enough to maintain interest but not so hard as to put players off."[20] With improved everything, digital innovations are "marrying the power of modern technology to the insatiable human desire for play." As every good Kindergarten teacher knows, learning cannot be far behind. Why can't schools be fun places to become immersed in learning? We are not there yet (remember we are still in the dreaming section), but we are getting awfully close to tasting it. We shape our tools and they shape us while we, in turn, re-shape them and so on.

There are some promising signs. We are making progress on assessing higher-order skills (HOS). It is hoped that Cisco-Intel-Microsoft will produce some concrete results in clarifying and assessing higher-order skills (alas, the pedagogical component will remain underdeveloped). In 2011, Nancy Watson and I completed a review for the Hewlett Foundation of their "deep learning" goals.[21] Their version of higher-order skills contains competencies organized into three categories: content knowledge (master core academic content, and acquire, apply, and expand knowledge); cognitive strategies (think critically, solve problems, and communicate effectively); and learning behaviors (work collaboratively, and learn how to learn).

The current focus in the United States typically revolves around the Common Core State Standards (CCSS). Forty-six states have signed on to focus on common core standards and their assessment in English Language Arts (ELA) and mathematics. These standards and assessments include higher-order skills. Much of the work funded by the federal government and prominent foundations is directed toward CCSS development. Hewlett has positioned itself to concentrate on the assessment of deep learning goals as a policy and practice chunk. It has some 30 grantees working on "proof points" of assessment of given competencies. While light on the pedagogical component, the results should help operationalize the meaning of specific deep learning competencies.

Similarly, the Bill & Melinda Gates Foundation, in addition to its high-profile work on assessing teacher effectiveness, is investing in a number of digitally based innovations to support new forms of student learning. Its report *Supporting Students: Investing in Innovation and Quality* outlines how the foundation has been investing in non-traditional projects such as "game-based applications and assessments."[22] In other cases it supports research "to better understand college-access and student persistence issues." The foundation is a first funder of our own solution—Motion Leadership/Madcap (MLM).

The Bill & Melinda Gates Foundation aspires to use technology and innovative instructional practices where "students learn beyond the bounds of traditional classrooms," and are investigating questions like these: "How can students engage in solving complex problems that are relevant to their lives? How can classroom design lead students to deep and enduring mastery of their schoolwork and skills? How can we capitalize on their digital prowess to inspire confidence, curiosity, persistence, and desire for knowledge?" Many of its grantees are basing innovations on digital tools that are participatory, engaging, co-creative, and collaborative. Gates has organized its investments into four categories: proficiency-based pathways; game-based assessments; digital course development; and college knowledge and academic tenacity. Once again we can expect some valuable concrete products from this work, but it will be small scale and may not develop the instructional practices as fully as we need.

There is one research project that links instructional practices to higher-order skills. It is Innovative Teaching and Learning (ITL), sponsored by Microsoft's Partners in Learning (PIL) initiative.[23] I have been involved in interpreting the ITL research findings. Using a simple but comprehensive framework, ITL examined four main variables: education system change (policy context); school leadership and culture; innovative teaching practices; and impact of student skills for life and work today. Researchers investigated classroom practices in a sample of PIL schools in seven countries: Australia, England, Finland, Indonesia, Mexico, Russia, and Senegal. I present only an overview of key findings for our purposes. Here are the findings in a nutshell:

1. Innovative teaching practices were identified as consisting of three elements: student-centered pedagogy (including knowledge building, self-regulation and assessment, collaboration, and skilled communication); extending learning beyond the classroom (including problem solving and real-world innovation); and Information and Communication Technology (ICT) use (in the service of specific and concrete learning goals).

2. Innovative teaching practices were more likely to be seen in schools where teachers collaborate in a focused way on the particular instructional practices linked explicitly to 21st century learning skills.

3. Innovative teaching was more frequent when teachers engaged in "professional development activities that involve the active and direct engagement of teachers," such as teachers conducting research or directly practicing new methods.

4. School leadership with vision and focus on supporting the development of ITL was found to be a key condition for implementation. Inclusion of innovative teaching in teacher appraisal was also a positive factor.

5. System focus and support (the largest element in the ecosystem model) was not only found to be missing, but current policies worked at cross purposes when narrow testing regimes conflicted with broader 21st century skills.

6. The above factors save for item 5 were linked to specific learning outcomes: knowledge building, use of ICT, problem solving and innovation, and skilled communication (collaboration could have been an outcome, but there was not enough evidence to assess it). The key is that when students experience innovative teaching practices, they are more likely to develop and demonstrate the skills needed for life and work.[24]

In one way these are pretty remarkable findings given that they come from a variety of situations, including several poor developing countries. For the first time we see a clear causal link between specific teaching practices and higher-order skills with technology figuring in a big way. What might be more remarkable is that this was accomplished without much deliberate system effort. Consider the following: "while we saw examples of innovative teaching practices in the classes we visited, a coherent and integrated set of conditions to support the adoption of innovative teaching was lacking in most of the schools and *all* of the systems in our sample."[25] Despite the fact that the sample explicitly sought innovative schools and innovative teachers, the findings show that only a sprinkling of innovative teachers are engaged in the practices found to be effective. In other words, we have ad hoc innovative teachers but not many innovative schools, and no innovative systems.

We see in the ITL research that individual and small groups of teachers can improve instructional practices that, in turn, affect higher-order learning outcomes, and that this process is strongly helped by the explicit use of digital technology for that purpose. More work needs to be done in the ITL project in order to flesh out what the new pedagogy looks like in practice. With this strong start the future of ITL will be worth following: the plan is to provide a framework and related tools for developing innovative teaching capacity and tying these practices to student work that promotes engagement in real-life problem solving and the development of higher-order thinking and living skills.

ITL is only a baby step, but it does begin to point the way. The argument in *Stratosphere* is this: imagine what could be accomplished if we integrated technology, pedagogy, and change knowledge on a large scale!

I mentioned that Ontario has had good success in improving literacy, numeracy, and high-school graduation. While some higher-order skills have improved, achievement results at the very top end (level 4 as assessed by our Education Quality and Accountability Office/EQAO) remained stuck at about 13 percent during this period. In 2010 we decided to address this issue in an innovative initiative, Student Work Study Teachers (SWST).

The SWST initiative is a Literacy and Numeracy Secretariat program structured around a collaborative study between an experienced practitioner working in a temporary research role, an SWS teacher, and a hosting classroom teacher. During the 2009–2010 school year, 50 SWS teachers from 19 district school boards across the province visited approximately 250 classrooms from Kindergarten to Grade 6. In 2010–2011, the initiative grew extensively with 75 SWS teachers from 54 district school boards across the province visiting about 765 classrooms from Kindergarten to Grade 6.

The focus of the SWST initiative is student learning and activity in the classroom, as opposed to teacher instructional activity. All conversation and actions within the study are based on what students are doing. The purpose of the SWST initiative is to learn more about the following:

- characteristics of student work at level 2 moving to levels 3 and 4
- kinds of feedback to students that result in improved work and engagement
- kinds of classroom conditions that support student learning

SWS teachers work with students predominantly related to four larger interrelated areas of pedagogy: rich and relevant tasks; student talk; gradual release of responsibility; and formative assessment.

The relationship between the host teacher and SWS teacher proved critical to the success of the initiative. Although relationships between SWS teachers and host teachers varied considerably among the participants, there is evidence that these relationships have become progressively more collaborative learning relationships. Aspects that became increasingly part of these relationships include information sharing, active learning by both the SWS teacher and host teacher, discussing findings, co-planning activities, co-analyzing evidence and observations, and meeting at informal/out-of-classroom times.

All SWS teachers indicated that students benefited as a result of participating in the initiative *sometimes*, while 88 percent of the SWS teachers indicated that students benefited as a result of participation *many times*. Similarly, 82 percent of the SWS teachers indicated that participating in this initiative as a researcher-practitioner influenced the ways they work as educators to a *large degree*, with another 19 percent indicating the same to *some degree*. All the SWS teachers also indicated that the initiative was an effective learning experience for host teachers involved in the initiative, with 40 percent of the SWS teachers reporting that it was also an effective learning experience for teachers not directly involved in the study but within the host schools.

The SWST initiative has begun to do some of the spadework that builds on students' own thinking and thus is representative of new pedagogy that gets at student engagement and alters the role of teacher toward orchestrator of learning. The 2011 research report shows that the SWST stance is having an impact on how teachers view their work: understanding student perspectives and preferences (greater personalization), matching strategies to student learning strengths and needs (greater precision), and teacher learning that arises from the analysis of student work (relevant professional learning). Participating teachers are concluding that they need to change their practice so that students are more actively engaged in learning with and from other students. SWST is also having an impact on how districts are organizing time and resources to support more inquiry-based professional learning. Moreover the improvement trajectory of schools where SWSTs were hosted is better than that of non-SWST schools as measured by EQAO results.

In terms of this book, SWST is doing all this with one hand tied behind its back in the sense that technology plays no particular role. The integration of technology will make this work easier, less expensive, and way more effective in its impact on higher-order skills learning.

All of these developments and more are pointing in the direction of being able to go deeper with students, of doing so on a very large scale, of making learning more interesting and engaging, and making the whole enterprise incredibly cheaper on a per capita basis. Stanford recently put three computer science courses online with scores of short videos with explanations of concepts and automatically graded exercises and made them available on the web. In the first month 300,000 students registered for the courses with millions of video views and thousands of submitted assignments.[26] The lecture is going to go the way of the dodo bird in postsecondary education, making universities much more effective and greatly reducing their spiraling costs (so that less money will be spent, and will be spent on better high-quality endeavors). In K–12 schools teacher talk will plummet, a good thing for teachers too since few of us like to talk when hardly anyone is listening. In the course of this development the roles of teachers and students are being flipped.

The Flipping of Teacher and Student Roles

Phil Schlechty has been arguing for some time that we must organize schools around the student as worker. Students take greater charge of their own and each other's learning and teachers become change agents. Instead of having students for a handful of hours per day at elementary school or a single period at high school, teachers could influence students indirectly 24/7. Students pursue stimulating learning via purposefully designed videos and games, and take up such learning in the classroom as well as with other students and teachers remotely.

More dodo birds. According to Schlechty, e-learning and all that surrounds it means that "the role of the teacher as instructor is obsolete."[27] New forms of engagement for students are the key. Work that meets the four criteria I set out at the beginning of this chapter is what needs to be designed—work that is irresistibly engaging, is elegantly easy to engage in, accesses technology ubiquitously, and is steeped in higher-order skills. With a bit of digital dreaming, we have seen in this chapter that there are distinct concrete products that are beginning to make all of this possible. To free up all that wasted instructional time is to generate a windfall of better time use, not to mention the new time that is created by the expansion of learning to the 24-hour clock and the hordes of peers engaged in collaborative social learning. Teachers in small groups become leaders, designers, and active guides to learning. Principals become leaders of leaders (not instructional leaders). District and state infrastructures become redesigned to promote and hold schools accountable to the kinds of innovative teaching and learning we saw in the ITL research (but in the actual case was missing, which is why the researchers did not find anything at scale).

John Hattie also comes to our rescue with his army of meta-studies. He too sees the effective teacher as active change agent. When he compared the effect sizes of instructional practices of "teacher as activator" (feedback to students, helping students access their own thinking, furnishing challenging goals and the like) with those of "teacher as facilitator" (problem-based learning, simulations and gaming, individualized instruction), the average effect sizes greatly favored the teacher as activator (0.60 to 0.17). Teacher as mere facilitator even with digital resources is not good enough. Learning must be palpably immersing and productive for students; teachers as change agents are responsible for helping to design that probability. Hattie found five important differences between expert teachers and average teachers. The former have high levels of knowledge and understanding of the subjects they teach; can guide learning to surface and deep outcomes; can successfully monitor learning and provide feedback that assists students in progress; can attend to more attitudinal attributes of learning (such as self-efficacy and mastery motivation); and can provide defensible evidence of positive impacts of the teaching on student learning.[28]

Hattie strongly argues that the most important aspect that a teacher must get good at is to know what impact he or she has on every student. All of the high-yield practices he found in his empirical analysis rely on the influence of student peers, feedback, transparent learning intentions, success criteria, and adjustment of instruction to attend to both surface and deep knowing. So the undisciplined possibilities of the web, no matter how wonderful, will not be sufficient. Unassisted discovery will be less likely to have benefits compared with the teacher as change agent who helps students learn how to learn and how to monitor their own learning.

Frankly, the current discussion about flipping the role of students and teachers is, to put it one way, flippant. We can't just go in and turn things upside down without a plan. We need clarity and precision. We need to get our pedagogy and our technology straight. Hattie helps a great deal, as does Prensky with his depiction of students and teachers as "partners in learning."[29] The next steps mean developing more examples on the ground and learning from them. Some help in this respect comes from another field, namely, the work from lean start-up in software development that I take up in Chapter 5. I introduce the analogy here.

Think of the teacher as manager and the students as the team. One concept in lean start-ups is "management with scrum" for agile learning, as depicted by Ken Schwaber. In Schwaber's *Agile Project Management with Scrum,* a Toyota leader provides a foreword that includes this insight: "the role of managers is to shape the organization not through the power of will or dictate, but rather through example, through coaching and through understanding and helping others to achieve their goals."[30] A good definition of the teacher and students in the new pedagogy!

The term *scrum* comes from rugby, and in learning, it means helping the team move forward when the direction is complex rather than straightforward. Again, think new pedagogy. The analogy to team is critical here. In education we are all attuned to personalization, or connecting with the needs of every learner in a way that can stoke the learner's passion and purpose. Yet with 25 or more students, it is a mathematical impossibility for a teacher to do this day after day. Teachers can do it, however, if they view their students as part of a team. The new pedagogy already is based on students working with one another and taking greater charge of their own learning, guided by the teacher as coach. Instead of thinking about how to differentiate instruction for each student, in the new essence-as-easy mode, the teacher needs to think of the class as a team and determine how to use the team to develop the team.

Think analogy again as you consider what Ryan Martens, founder of Rally Software, said at a meeting we had at the Massachusetts Institute of Technology. The topic: capacity building. Martens said, "People in our industry have learned that it is all about rapid learning cycles, fast feedback, continual reflection, good coaching, and managers who create conditions for learning rather than try to make it happen."[31] Can you think of a better rendition of the new pedagogy we are exploring in this book? Likely not. Teacher as change agent and coach; teacher as developer of individuals and team; teacher as catalyst for increasingly self-sufficient learners—in the learning organization, manager as leader and teacher as leader are one and the same. This relationship is exactly what Hattie and Prensky are getting at as they provide concrete examples of what the new pedagogy looks like in practice. It is not vague flipping but highly disciplined learning at work.

We also see more fleshed-out versions of the new learning complete with the flipped roles in Wagner's examples of the development of the eight innovators he profiles in *Creating Innovators*. Note his subtitle: *The Making of Young People Who Will Change the World*. In each case the students in question were permitted and guided to their purpose, passion, and play in life by parents and/or serendipitous mentors. They were given freedom and guidance. In every case the students got less from all their regular classes combined compared to the creative outlets they ended up pursuing. Wagner makes the case that young people by and large want to make an impact but that their potential lies dormant or often gets thwarted by traditional schooling. What would it mean, he wonders,

> if we were to intentionally develop the entrepreneurial and innovative talents of all young people—to nurture their initiative, curiosity, imagination, creativity, and collaborative skills, as well as their analytical abilities, along with essential qualities of character such as persistence, empathy and strong moral foundation?[32]

I mentioned earlier Kirk Phelps, one of Wagner's five STEM innovators. The breakthrough for Phelps came when he took a Smart Product Design course with Ed Carryer at Stanford. Carryer was not a tenured faculty member, but more of a hybrid. Interested in how to build stuff, he became the young man's teacher and mentor. Carryer talks about the essential elements of educating young people to become innovators: "the value of hands-on projects where students have to solve a real problem and demonstrate mastery; the importance of learning to draw on academic content from multiple disciplines to solve a problem; learning to work in teams."[33] Such learning and involvement can occur for all students as Wagner illustrated whether they are into STEM type product design like Kirk Phelps, or social justice innovations as we saw with Laura White at Tulane University. In all cases the student is empowered to learn, but the teacher guides and mentors to develop the intrinsic motivation and creative thinking and doing skills—flipped roles in action. This is just like Robinson's mentors who recognized, encouraged, facilitated, and stretched their protégées.

On a global level we see many more examples of students involved in learning applied skills while working on real-life problems in Microsoft's Innovative Schools program and related spinoffs. Addressing deforestation is attracting involvement among young people around the world, and it has all the trappings of the new pedagogy. In March 2010 Toronto's Michael Furdyk helped launch DeforestACTION though his TakingITGlobal (TIG) network. The project began at the Microsoft Asia Pacific Partners in Learning Program "with the goal of empowering learners to take control of the planet they will inherit, while developing the most important 21st century learning skills."[34] Over 80,000 students from more than 60 countries are developing as global citizens by collaborating to solve global problems; reviewing and evaluating the causes, impact, and politics of deforestation at the local and global levels; analyzing, planning, and organizing by using collaborative technology; preparing and implementing action plans by engaging in interactive activities; and taking part in valuable conversations with peers and mentors.

For one example of what can be done within a few years, see the work of Willie Smits, the Dutch biologist who took residence in Borneo and became an Indonesian citizen. Smits helped the local community reclaim vast tracks of destroyed land, transforming it within five years to a vibrant sustainable ecosystem with priceless benefits: arable land, local jobs, marketable products, and better lives for all. To take the flip side of the equation: at the beginning there was one large community that was devastated by deforestation, the land useless. Within one year of the forest fires that caused the deforestation, no children gained any weight, while they lost 12 IQ points—in a single year![35]

As exciting as these examples are, we are talking about exceptions to the rule. They are the first disruptive examples on the road to a radical and achievable new future. The solutions are not all that elusive. We currently have many ad hoc examples where students and teachers work together to go deeply into hands-on learning involving real-life matters with technology playing a starring role. These examples are becoming more and more successful in developing 21st century learning skills and commitments.

One can see this in full bloom in model schools such as High Tech High in San Diego, a well-documented illustration of what can be accomplished.[36] The problem with High Tech High, even though it is an exciting and undisputed success, is that it is atypical and unique in its set-up. Because of this, and using my ease of use criterion, I prefer to examine ordinary schools with run-of-the-mill resources transforming themselves, and thus being able to show other schools how possible (easy) and how deeply compelling it is to go down this path. For that reason, I turn to Park Manor, a public elementary school in Ontario.

Park Manor is a senior public school, with 300 students in Grades 6 to 8, located just west of Toronto in the town of Elmira.[37] When you examine their focus, "Park Manor's Accelerated Learning Framework," you would swear that they had based their work on *Stratosphere* (they didn't; I wrote the first draft of this book before I knew about Park Manor). It's all there! Their core goal is to develop "global critical thinkers collaborating to change the world." The framework (Exhibit 4.3 on next page) is surrounded by "digitally rich learning tasks without limits." It integrates technological tools, exemplary pedagogy, rich learning tasks, and 21st century learning skills.

At Park Manor it is clear that pedagogy is the driver with student learning at the center and technology as the Formula 1 Grand Prix machine that gets the student there faster and better. Using the Accelerated Learning Framework, each teacher and each student can articulate the learning goal and the success criteria, why and how they are using a particular technological tool, and how the use of the tool meets the student learning need.

Whether the learning goal involves creating an iMovie to raise awareness about global issues, completing a writing task by making inferences and using graphic organizers to sort out and convey ideas, or helping a

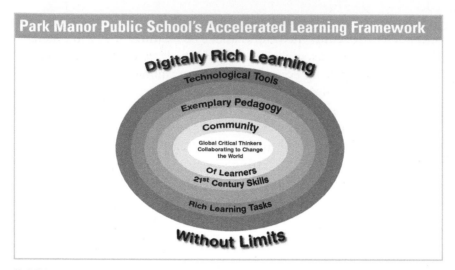

Exhibit 4.3

student new to Canada learn English, the Accelerated Learning Framework is the same. The technological tools used at Park Manor include PlayBooks, computers, iPads, and Document Cameras—the framework is amenable for use with any advanced digital equipment.

The school uses success criteria and evidence to determine the effectiveness of the framework as it relates to student learning. The success criteria explain in detail how students and teachers can determine that the technology tool, program, application, or website adds value to student learning. They pertain to student engagement, active learning, easier learning, assessment *for* learning (student feedback), assessment *as* learning (students monitoring their own learning), assessment *of* learning (concrete evidence), 21st century learning skills (creating, collaborating, communicating, critical thinking, and citizenship), support for higher-yield instructional strategies (differentiated learning and gradual acceptance of responsibility), and finally, easier instruction (for the teacher).

These success criteria are then linked to "evidence of accomplishment" (what success looks and sounds like; what students are doing, saying, or producing). Next, the school assesses how much accelerated learning is occurring as a result of the technology. It does so according to three measures: Does the technology in question enable the student to Meet (M) the success criteria? Does it help the student get there Faster (F)? And does it assist the student in achieving Higher (H) levels of learning than he or she would without using the particular technology? (This question is answered by comparing how individual students respond to an activity with or without technology, noting how to increase engagement, speed, and quality of learning and achievement.) These three questions, unlike most accounts, directly focus on determining the relative role of technology in student success.

Park Manor has posted dramatic gains on Ontario's assessment system concerning the percentage of students achieving levels 3 and 4— high standards that reflect higher-order skills. In writing, for example, from 2007 to 2011, scores for Grade 6 students increased from 44 percent to 78 percent (for boys, the gains were 32 percent to 72 percent). This increase cannot be attributed to the use of technology, which began in earnest in 2009. Likely though, it is the result of teachers' intentional focus on improving writing through the use of success criteria and exemplary pedagogy buttressed by greater use of technology. Technology serves to accelerate and deepen learning.

Clearly, Park Manor represents "human *using* machine" rather than the reverse. Co-creators of the framework, Principal James Bond and teacher Liz Anderson, explain it this way:

> Since September 2009 our staff has been engaged in a change process that has taken us from no classroom technology to a digitally rich learning environment through the collaborative development of the framework, its activation, and now its assessment. We believe that if we are going to invest money, time and other resources in purchasing and integrating technology it needs to be hugely value added with respect to student learning. Moreover it needs to lead to the development of 21st century skills and ways of thinking required by students to be global critical citizens who can help change the world for the better.

Other schools in the region are showing an increasing interest in what Park Manor is doing. Bond and Anderson report that such schools are finding the Accelerated Learning Framework practical and easy to enact. Moreover, they say, "it is flexible enough to implement in a variety of settings—high school, elementary, special education." In short, we are talking about an innovation that may be "irresistibly engaging" and "elegantly easy to use": one that produces powerful learning results.

I chose Park Manor to feature because it is a normal school with standard resources—just like any of the 120 schools in the Waterloo school district. It has no special status or privileges. It has gone from a situation of using no technology to the vibrant integration of technology and pedagogy in just two and a half years. Its success shows that stratospheric scenarios are practical and compelling.

Still, stratosphere won't be satisfied until 100 percent of the schools in the district are so engaged and 100 percent of the districts in the province are integrating pedagogy and technology and achieving great buy-in and ownership.

Whether we are talking about an engaging program such as DeforestACTION or the initiative of a small school to promote the development of global critical citizens, we can begin to appreciate the potential of the new pedagogy. All the 21st century learning skills and qualities can be served at once: passion, purpose, problem solving, creativity, skilled communication, collaboration, technological savvy, citizenship, expertise, and sustainability. Learning becomes more engrossing for students, and teaching becomes easier and more consequential for teachers. The learner benefits; the world benefits. Stratosphere is a synergistic innovation.

In short, we need to create the new digital learning reality on a massive scale—for *all* students and teachers. I believe that this expansion—or more accurately, multiple parallel developments merging and converging—can happen rapidly in the next few years. Pedagogy is becoming sharper and more penetrating; technology is becoming mightier and easier to use and integrate.

One more ingredient is needed to complete the assault: the growing clarity and power of design and change knowledge that will be essential for achieving reform on a large scale—whole-system reform. The reason we need change knowledge is that the revolution I am addressing is *within* the public school system. I am not calling for an end run—but a revamping of the system we have. It is true that the system won't be recognizable. It is true that the boundaries will become outwardly limitless. But it will still be us—all of us. Boredom will be the least of our worries!

Design Principles and Change Knowledge

Aside from being a hard-ass, Steve Jobs knew the skinny of successful change. It is amazing how the design principles for successful products and what we know about leading whole-system reform are converging. We begin with the former.

Design Principles for Successful Products

Walter Isaacson has written a wonderful biography of Steve Jobs.[1] Early in the book Isaacson identifies a theme that captures what *Stratosphere* strives for in its digital world—sophisticated design combined with irresistible, engrossing ease of use as you acquire deep learning competencies at an affordable cost. Jobs talks about his passion from an early age for making nicely designed products (which he later called "insanely great") for the mass market: "I love it when you can bring really great design and simple capability to something that doesn't cost much."[2]

The first investor that Jobs attracted when Apple was not yet formed in 1976 was Mike Markkula, a 33-year-old retired entrepreneur who had made millions in stock options at Intel. Markkula proposed that he and Jobs first draft a business plan, most of which Markkula wrote. The result was a marvelous example of the skinny—"The Apple Marketing Philosophy," a one pager based on three principles (now familiar to us in our motion leadership work):

The first was *empathy*, an intimate connection with the feelings of the customer: "We will fully understand their needs better than any other company." The second was *focus*: "In order to do a good job of those things that we decide to do, we must eliminate all of the unimportant opportunities." The third and equally important principle, awkwardly named, was *impute*. It emphasized that people form an opinion about a company or product based on the signals that it conveys… "We may have the best product, the highest quality, the most useful software etc.; if we present them in a slipshod manner, they will be perceived as slipshod; if we present them in a creative, professional manner, we will *impute* the desired qualities."[3]

For the rest of his career, Jobs would understand the needs and desires of customers, focus on a handful of core products, and obsess with the image and details of marketing and packaging. "When you open the box of an iPhone or iPad, we want that tactile experience to set the tone for how you perceive the product," Jobs said at a later point.[4] Another compatible concept close to Jobs's design philosophy from the early days was the maxim attributed to Leonardo da Vinci: "Simplicity is the ultimate sophistication." This maxim was on Apple's very first brochure.

When Apple was incorporated in 1977, it was valued at $5,309. By December 1980 it came in at $1.79 billion! In 1984 Bill Gates said: "To create a new standard takes not just making something that's a little bit different, it takes something that's really new and captures people's imagination. And the Macintosh, of all the machines I've ever seen, is the only one that meets that standard."[5] Jobs would continue to meet that standard in the ensuing years whether he was outside the company (as he was from 1985 to 1997) or back in control. From the Macintosh launch in 1984 to the iPad in 2010, empathy, focus, and presentation would be Jobs's trademark.

More simplicity. In 1987 IBM offered to license the NeXT software that Jobs had created and sent him a 125-page contract. Jobs never read it, responding, "You don't get it." He demanded a much shorter contract and he got it within a week.[6]

Steve Jobs then had his bout with the integration of creativity and technology in the animated film business with Pixar and Walt Disney Studios, *Toy Story*, and so on. When he returned to Apple in 1997 the company had lost its empathy, focus, impute center. In his first year back, he cut 70 percent of the products under development. At a key meeting,

He grabbed a magic marker, padded to a whiteboard, and drew a horizontal and vertical line to make a four-squared chart. "Here's what we need," he continued. Atop the two columns he wrote "Consumer" and "Pro"; he labeled the two rows "Desktop" and "Portable." Their job, he said, was to make four great products, one for each quadrant.[7]

"This ability to focus saved Apple," Isaacson writes.[8]

Jobs had the ability along the way to link up with a few key people who complemented and deepened his grasp of sophisticated simplicity (Steve Wozniak in the early days, for example). One of these people was Jonathan Ive, who was head of Apple's design team as Jobs returned in 1997. Ive was on the verge of quitting because Apple had lost its way. Jobs convinced him to stay with the promise that "our goal is not just to make money but to make great products."[9] Together they captured Kluger's *simplexity*, another watchword that has become the basis of our motion leadership work.[10] Focus on a small number of ambitious goals and factors (the simple part) and make them gel—get the chemistry right between people and products (the complex part).

Jobs and Ive together worked out the simplexity balance. From the beginning Jobs had aimed for "the simplicity of conquering complexities not ignoring them," observes Isaacson. In Jobs's own words, "It takes a lot of hard work to make something simple, to truly understand the underlying challenges and come up with elegant solutions."[11] Jonathan Ive describes his philosophy:

Why do we assume that simple is good? Because with physical products, we have to feel that we dominate them. As you bring order to complexity, you find a way to make the product defer to you. Simplicity isn't just a visual style. It's not just minimalism or the absence of clutter. It involves digging through the depth of the complexity. To be truly simple, you have to go really deep. For example, to have no screws on something, you can end up having a product that is so convoluted and so complex. The better way is to go deeper with the simplicity, to understand everything about it and how it's manufactured. You have to deeply understand the essence of a product in order to be able to get rid of the parts that are not essential.[12]

Or Jobs again, telling *Fortune*, "In most people's vocabularies, design means veneer. But to me, nothing could be further from the meaning of design. Design is the fundamental soul of a man-made creation that ends up expressing itself in successive outer layers."[13] Despite Jobs's hard side and autocratic nature when it came to designing products, the process was highly collaborative and iterative among the designers, the product developers, the engineers, and the manufacturing team. Lots of meetings, going back frequently to the beginning, constantly asking, "Do we need that part?" There followed the iMac, Apple stores, iTunes, the iPod (including the brilliantly simple scroll). Isaacson notes that consumers ensured the success of the iPod. Beyond that, the iPod came to epitomize everything Apple: "poetry connected to engineering, arts and creativity intersecting with technology, design that's bold and simple."[14] The new integration means loving both technology and artistry.

Designers are attracted by the elegance of things. They are drawn to create things that no one else has done, and to develop products or services that allow us to do things we love in a way that could never have been enjoyed before. They are intrinsically motivated to invent things that they and the world find delectable. Like master chefs they gain most pleasure when others consume their creations. Money is a by-product.

Then came the iPad, which appears to make a great leap forward for our technology-pedagogy-change trio. This story from Michael Noer seems to support that.

> Noer was reading a science fiction novel on his iPad while staying at a dairy farm in a rural area north of Bogotá, Colombia, when a poor six-year-old boy who cleaned the stables came up to him. Curious, Noer handed him the device. With no instruction, and never having seen a computer before, the boy started using it intuitively. He began swiping the screen, launching apps, playing a pinball game. "Steve Jobs has designed a powerful computer that an illiterate six-year-old can use without instruction," Noer wrote. "If that isn't magical, I don't know what is."[15]

Apple sold one million iPads in less than a month, 15 million in nine months. Moses and the two tablets of the Ten Commandments aside, this tablet marks the beginning of ubiquitous technology, bringing us closer and closer to essence as easy—for *all*. And it really is just a new beginning: Apps Unlimited.

Even orangutans are getting into the act. In one experiment sponsored by Microsoft in the jungles of Indonesia, an orangutan learned how to take pictures from an iPad in less than a minute and proceeded to go on a photo-taking binge. In the experiment, the apes work through a cage because they tend to destroy the machine if given it on their own—another design problem for Apple to solve? In any case, we are not too far off from apes lining up to buy iPads.

Be that as it may, the education revolution is not a given. The first is that even the most sophisticated technology still needs to be guided by strong pedagogy. In this respect even the vaunted iPad doesn't measure up. Orrin Murray and Nicole Olcese review the iPad from a teaching and learning perspective. They conclude that technological companies and leading policy makers are seduced by the apparent power of ever inno-vating technological products. To get a PDA (personal digital assistant) in every child's hands seems so evidently desirable. Another silver bullet wasted if you don't concentrate on best pedagogy. Just to take one minor example: developers do not focus on collaboration that takes advantage of the capabilities of the device and its operating systems. Recall the Cana-dian study that kids these days are technological whizzes when it comes to the tool, but pedagogically clueless with respect to getting the best out of it. Murray and Olcese eventually draw the following conclusion:

> We cannot point to a single application that steps up to modern understanding of how people learn. Our study suggests that there is a paucity of applications that truly extend capability... the lack of collaboration capabilities underlie this point, as do the overwhelming number of applications that are simply drill and practice or focused on delivering content for consumption, not creation or re-use.[16]

Still, there is no denying that good technology under the direction of a great pedagogue can do wonders. Take my colleague David Booth, professor of literacy if there ever was one, who is always trying to engage young people, especially boys, in reading. He sent me this account:

iPad Literacy

A school in Timmins, a mining community in Northern Ontario, is part of our research project exploring literacy devel-opment through the incorporation of iPads into the daily reading and writing events of an all-boys classroom. With each student being supplied with an iPad for the year, we set up the e-resources that would act as a library of novels as well as research suggestions for organizing some of the units the students would explore. I visited the class as a guest teacher, where I demon-strated some of the literacy strategies that the iPad could support in promoting both the reading of information and fiction texts, and the enriching and expansion of the big ideas that inquiry facilitates. I wasn't prepared for the power that technology puts in the hands of the youngsters, and I became part of the learning process with the boys and their teacher, caught up in the ease and accessibility of the world of information that this wireless tool can offer even amateurs like me. The boys were given some hands-on workshops by the technology consultant, and within moments had found the games that connect them to the pop culture of the techno generation, and swiped their way across the screens into more text forms than I knew existed.

For the next demonstration, I wanted to explore research strategies using the Internet with the iPads. I asked the boys to find information on the Internet about a hero that interested them. I wrote their responses on the SMART Board, and they ranged from Batman to Terry Fox to JFK. As the list grew longer, I asked the boys to classify their responses into categories, and they came up with political heroes, celebrities, artists, sports heroes, war heroes, people who demonstrated courage, and when one boy shouted out "Jesus," we added religious heroes. The lists they had discovered on the Internet could not have been found in any one reference book, and they dug deeper and deeper into what defines a hero.[17]

More e-learning is being unleashed. The move by Apple to turn textbooks into e-books, even with iBooks Author and manipulation options, aggravates the problem of technology as seductive because the technology *looks* so great. It never *is* great unless guided by a wise pedagogue. Mostly, as we have seen, technology has a life and market of its own. We need to figure out the new role of teachers in this new learning equation. The scariest part about the new technologies is that they give people the false sense that they are learning something just by using an elegant machine.

The next time you marvel at your 18-month-old granddaughter working away through some iPad apps and routines, remind yourself that it may be no more impressive than what an ape can do (this still may be a compliment). More seriously, there is no question that this toddler will grow up to be a whiz at using technology. But how well she learns to work her way through the 21st century will depend on whether she encounters great pedagogy and mentors along the way. Technological prowess by itself doesn't make you much smarter (although it may appear to).

Pedagogy, powering 21st century skills, is what will make the difference. This realization is probably what has caused South Korea to stop and rethink its digital expansion. Already one of the top five performing countries in the world in education, South Korea is questioning the wisdom of its commitment to digitize all of its elementary, middle, and high schools by 2015. It originally thought that complete digitization would turn the country into a "knowledge powerhouse" breeding students equipped for the future.[18]

Not so fast, its current leaders seem to say! Smartphone–obsessed students are not necessarily smarter and may suffer from the kind of internet addiction we saw earlier from Rosen (in South Korea a government survey found that 1 in 12 students between the ages of five and nine were addicted to the internet). Now the country will proceed more cautiously—assessing, for example, the results of 50 pilot schools that are using technology more fully before deciding on next steps. The Korean leaders seem to know that it is folly to introduce digital textbooks on a massive scale without having a solid pedagogical plan to go with it.

My point is not to halt technology but to consider how to integrate it with learning, and this is where we will clash with existing education cultures. When in 2006 David Williamson Shaffer wrote *How Computer Games Help Children Learn*, he built his case on how the games can be played out of school.[19] Shaffer figured that the way schools are organized makes it too difficult for computers to be used effectively. Such end runs are unfortunate in light of the fact that the games featured by Shaffer focus on "making and applying knowledge"—that is, the new pedagogy—instead of learning facts, information, and theories in the abstract.

So, why might it be different this time? We have some hope—indeed, it is why I wrote this book—because we know more about the new pedagogy, and the machines are getting better. If we can marry the two, we may produce creative learners in vast numbers. The fact that we are at the early stages relative to Christensen and Raynor's "disruptive innovation" paradigm (at the beginning of a new improvement cycle) gives us more reasons to be optimistic.

I don't think that Steve Jobs would have solved the problem of linking great pedagogy with great technology. Isaacson reports, "Jobs was somewhat dismissive of the idea that technology could transform education."[20] Somehow I don't think that Jobs would have had the temperament to get through the first meeting with school people on the topic. However, he did have his sights on the textbook industry:

He believed it was an $8 billion a year industry ripe for digital destruction. He was also struck by the fact that many schools, for security reasons, don't have lockers, so kids have to lug a heavy backpack around. "The iPad would solve that," he said. His idea was to hire great textbook writers to create digital versions, and make them a feature of the iPad.[21]

This is in fact where Apple is heading.

But, as I have laid out in *Stratosphere*, we can do much better than great online textbooks. Empathy, focus, and impute, and you have the non-linear dynamism of Park Manor Public School and many of the other iDream, iDo innovations now under way. Jobs partly anticipated the scenario of student as knowledge worker and teacher as change agent.

> It was absurd, he added, that American classrooms were still based on teachers standing at a board and using textbooks. All books, learning materials, and assessments should be digital and interactive, tailored to each student and providing feedback in real time.[22]

He, too, was about flipping the role of students and teachers, although I suspect he might have wanted to flip the teacher right out of the picture.

Jobs saw that the iPad and its successors were not just tablets and those imitating them as such were missing the point. "It's in Apple's DNA," he said in March 2011 at the launch of iPad2, "that technology alone is not enough. We believe that it's technology married with the humanities that yields us the result that makes our heart sing."[23] Yes, humanities—the creative arts as we have seen with Sir Ken Robinson, but Jobs omitted to introduce the role of proactive pedagogy.

Near the end of his life Jobs said that in relation to its customers, Apple's role "is to figure out what they're going to want before they do"[24]: another design principle he anticipated as we are about to see from Adrian Slywotzky. In *Demand: Creating What People Love Before They Know They Want It*.[25] Slywotzky examines a number of rapidly successful innovations, from CareMore health to Zipcar, and finds that they have six things in common. The innovations are magnetic, hassle free, have strength of backstory, and focus on trigger, trajectory, and variation.

Demand creators spend a lot of time trying to understand people (Apple's empathy). They don't stop developing their product until it's "absolutely irresistible." They *impute* magnetism, to use Apple's verb, "generating excitement and conversation everywhere."[26]

The demand creators "fix the hassle map" (our elegant ease of use). They set out to reduce all the annoyances and time and money wasters—Steve Jobs didn't even like on-off switches because there was one click too many. They also "build a complete backstory"—the sophistication and ingenuity are in the design in order to make use smooth. They try to anticipate everything in the design and get it right in the first place.

These change designers seek "to find the triggers" that are the key to takeoff use. The biggest obstacles to change are inertia, skepticism, and indifference. The product and the process have to overcome these stalwarts of the status quo. They don't just launch into the market with front-end fanfare, but see it as only the first step "to build a steep trajectory." Again, keeping it simple and focused. How fast can we get better in both technical (the product) and emotional (relating to users) dimensions?

Finally, they plan for purposeful variation, what Slywotzky calls "de-average." They know that one size does not fit all, but endless variation is not an option. They try to meet the needs of different types of users, that is, to personalize.

Zipcar worked because the designers figured out that making cars available five minutes from home compared to 15 or even 10 minutes made a huge difference. Slywotzky concludes that "great demand creators eliminate or reduce the hassles that make most products and services inconvenient, costly, unpleasant, and frustrating."[27]

We can understand cars and groceries, but what about something more difficult such as selling symphony subscriptions (or improving education)? The key to developing services or products that sell is that the innovation must focus on the customer, not the device (remember the milkshake mistake in Chapter 2). To get more people to symphonies or to medical appointments, do something simple, like offer free parking or free transportation. Make sure that you have a magnetic product, though, as well as skilled professionals who care about what they do.

One group consisting of nine symphonies in nine different cities decided to find out more about their customers. Slywotzky describes how they improved attendance at their concerts not just by focusing on the quality of their performances, but also by figuring out the "demand variation" of existing and potential audiences (this is variation, de-averaging, or personalization). Customer variation is not endless, but it is more than one group. This research found that an incredible 91 percent of first-time concertgoers did not come back. When the researchers looked more closely, they found six different customer types: core audience, trialists, the non-committed (a few concerts), special occasion attendees, snackers (regulars who purchase subsets of tickets each year), and high potentials (people who attend quite a few concerts but have not purchased subscriptions). At the top of the hassle map for most groups was parking. So was the no refunds, no exchange policy.

Trajectory is continuous improvement. Slywotzky reports that Aldous Huxley's favorite motto was "nothing short of everything is ever really enough."[28]

That's about it. Always trying to figure out what people want (even before they do) and making it easy for them to experience it hassle free and as something irresistibly engaging (how about schools becoming hassle free and engaging?). Slywotzky says that the Achilles heel of demand is the launch of the product. Most innovators feel that their product is the real McCoy yet 80 percent of new businesses fail. Product development or service development must meet the criteria we have been discussing in this chapter, which includes getting it as right as right can be to begin with. If the emerging product is not magnetic, demand creators will stop production if they have to. Then after the launch it is essential to stay close to the customer—emotionally and technically. Hassle free and high yield all the way.

Slywotzky takes up the future of demand, reporting on a 2008 survey from the National Academy of Engineering, whose members were asked to name the "Grand Challenges of the 21st Century." The top five:

1. Make solar energy economical

2. Provide energy from fusion

3. Provide access to clean water

4. Reverse-engineer the brain

5. Advance personalized learning[29]

These were engineers. No doubt doctors would have curing cancer near the top of their priorities. But I would venture to say that almost every group would have the integration of technology, human and social learning, and the improvement of the world in their top 10.

Finally from a design perspective, Eric Ries in the *The Lean Startup* provides a valuable perspective for innovations at the early disruptive stage. These innovations by definition have not yet been worked out. True to the new pedagogy, Ries says we have to develop them through an iterative process by creating, trying, refining, applying, and continuously improving them in practice—in real situations—rather than trying to perfect them in the lab prior to trial.

Ries, like our skinny aspirations, has a simple three-part model: vision, steer, and accelerate. The directional vision is a crucial starting point, but you don't really know where it will take you until you experiment, refine, and what Ries calls "steer." Once you know what you are doing at the operational level, you accelerate. The general idea, says Ries, is that instead of spending years perfecting our technology, we build a "minimum viable product," or (MVP), that is imperfect, to say the least. Build, measure, learn is the notion (but know that you have to have a pretty good idea—vision—to begin with). Ries contends that "the lean startup is a new way of looking at the development of innovative new products that emphasizes fast iteration and customer insight, a huge vision, and great ambition, all at the same time."[30] Think of the task as creating an MVP which you develop through subsequent validated learning, recommends Ries.

In this way of thinking, strategy is a means of developing a new product, not implementing one. This approach is especially suited to situations of uncertainty and intense competition. What differentiates the success stories from the failures according to Ries is that "the successful entrepreneurs had the foresight, the ability, and the tools to discover which parts of their plans were working brilliantly and which were misguided, and adapt their strategies accordingly."[31]

One of Ries's colleagues, Ash Maurya, provides more practical lean advice in *Running Lean: Iterate from Plan A to a Plan That Works*. Maurya's idea is that when we work in new territory (as in schools integrating pedagogy and technology), the innovative cycle is about "speed, learning, and focus"; "engaging customers [learners] throughout the product development cycle"; and continually "testing a vision."[32] This learning/development process is not about advance testing through focus groups (people don't know what they have never experienced). Rather, much like Steve Jobs's approach, it is about uncovering and discovering desires not yet fully formed, about creating new realities by being close to the learner.

The reader will note that the views of Ries and Maurya are somewhat at odds with Apple's philosophy of perfecting the design before releasing it with fanfare, but Apple has been building on successes that were already proven to a certain extent. The notion that you "steer" when you don't quite know what you are doing and are in unpredictable waters, and you accelerate when you are in open waters and you know more is perfectly compatible with life in the stratosphere.

In this chapter we have been encroaching more and more onto our third domain of the integrated solution. Technology and the pedagogy are the first two—change knowledge is the third. Like the new pedagogy, valuable change knowledge has an action bias—like vision, steer, accelerate; like ready-fire-aim. Let's take a closer look at what we have been learning about change.

Change Knowledge

Change knowledge is a curious phrase. We have been working on it for almost four decades. Change knowledge is about implementation, which is putting something new into practice. Quality implementation is key. To implement successfully on a large scale is whole-system reform. There is no point integrating technology and pedagogy into a great new product if it falters due to superficial or poor implementation. Even things that turn out to be good for us often daunt us at the beginning. It is normal to fear change and to feel awkward around the simplest new thing. Thus, people need support and sometimes a nudge or push to try new things. This is where change knowledge comes in. It can make all the difference in the world. It can make the difference between technology working for or against us. Change knowledge enables us to more accurately assess whether a particular new thing is worthwhile or not. Making this judgment means getting inside the change process. Fortunately, we know a lot about the process of change, and this knowledge is essential any time we are around technology.

Progress for us is simplexity. We call it "motion leadership" or the skinny on becoming change savvy. Motion leadership is about leadership that causes positive movement forward for individuals, organizations, and entire systems. The change knowledge you need to do this must meet four criteria: (1) motivate people to engage in deep meaningful change, even when they might not want to do it at the outset; (2) help them learn from wrong paths and blind alleys; (3) use the group; and (4) do all of this on a very large scale (whole-system reform). In order to do this, change knowledge has to meet the design criteria we have been addressing in this chapter. In this section I try to make change knowledge more explicit. Exhibit 5.1 contains our skinny list. Pedagogy and technology provide the directional vision; change knowledge helps us achieve it, learning while we go.

The first thing to say is that all eight aspects must be addressed and connected. We have seen the importance of *focus* throughout this book. We have established the need to focus on a small number of ambitious priorities and stay the course, going ever wider and deeper. Focus saved Apple; it could save us.

These days the big need in education is to make it more engaging, capturing the deep learning or higher-order skills goals, raising the bar, and closing the gap in given societies and the world as a whole. Addressing this focus requires immersion in real life–change problems and the

Exhibit 5.1 Change Knowledge	
1.	Focus
2.	Innovation
3.	Empathy
4.	Capacity building
5.	Contagion
6.	Transparency
7.	Elimination of non-essentials
8.	Leadership

solving of many of them. Technology plays a big role, but not as an aimless powerhouse.

Focus is also about getting the roles right, especially by recasting those of student and teacher. I suspect that Steve Jobs would have and Bill Gates will likely support freeing up students so they can access information more easily and more widely, but doing this is only half the solution. In May 2011,

> Jobs asked some questions about education, and Gates sketched out his vision of what schools in the future would be like, with students watching lectures and video lessons on their own while using the classroom time for discussions and problem solving. They agreed that computers had, so far, made surprisingly little impact on schools—far less than on other realms of society such as media and medicine and law. For that to change, Gates said, computers and mobile devices would have to focus on delivering more personalized lessons and providing motivational feedback.[33]

This vision is incomplete for our stratosphere agenda because it omits pedagogy—*it omits the teacher!* The teacher as change agent is crucial, or we will get aimless multi-tasking. That six-year-old illiterate boy in Bogota did remarkably well on his own with the iPad, but he would do so much better if led by a skilled change agent teacher. Your 18-month-old granddaughter, as mentioned earlier, might become a whiz at the iPad; however, she will fizzle without skilled teachers and mentors. The skills of teacher as change agent are now known. John Hattie, 800 meta-studies later, concludes that "critical change agents (in order) are knowledge and skills; a plan of action; strategies to overcome setbacks; a high sense of confidence; monitoring progress; a commitment to achieve; social and environment support; and, finally, freedom, control, or choice."[34]

In a follow-up book Hattie stresses that the main preoccupation of teachers must be to constantly figure out how "to know thine impact." Teachers' fundamental task, says Hattie, is "to evaluate the effect of their teaching on students' learning and achievement" and "to believe that success and failure in student learning is about what they as teachers or leaders did or did not do."[35] We, the teachers, are change agents, he almost shouts! Learning, not teaching per se, is the measure. The new pedagogy flips the role of students and teachers where students are knowledge workers, learning to learn and think better, and where teachers see assessment as feedback about their impact and engage in dialogue with students about their aspirations and progress. As we saw in Chapter 3, this may turn out to be easier than we think—essence as easy where learning becomes win-win for teachers and students alike. Lyn Sharratt and I have also spelled out such a scenario in *Putting FACES on the Data*.[36]

In short, technology and pedagogy must be integrated around the roles of *both* students and teachers. This is the essence of focus for the future of education. The bored student and the alienated teacher gain a new lease on life. Schooling and education become what they are meant to be in the 21st century.

Second, we need to use the design criteria in this chapter and the four criteria at the beginning of Chapter 4 to develop and support digitally based curriculum *innovations* that are irresistible. I won't repeat the details here, but I'll note that this challenge can be met with increasing momentum. It will be dramatically better and markedly cheaper—a better proposition you could not find.

Third, *empathy* is turning out to be a rich, multi-faceted resource. It is so much more than understanding and identifying with others as if you were in their shoes. Our change work demonstrates that great teachers and other leaders respect others before the latter have earned it (in order to begin the change process), and have *impressive* empathy, or understanding of others who are in their way (that's why it is impressive). And as we have seen in this chapter, leadership and teaching is proactive in the sense of helping other people create a world they didn't know they wanted. What could be a better description of teaching than that!

Teachers then are essential. We just need different ones en masse than we have now. In our book *Professional Capital*, Andy Hargreaves and I have mapped out in detail what the professional capital of teachers would look like.[37] Hargreaves and I believe we need to foster a combination of human capital, social capital (focused teamwork), and decisional capital—and we need to do so in the entire teaching force. We have provided action pathways to get there, although we did not take up how technology could accelerate this process.

We are now talking about our fourth critical change factor: ongoing *capacity building*. Capacity building consists of the knowledge, skills, and dispositions of individuals and groups relative to the ability to do something according to a high standard. Because there is so much to learn in the stratosphere (it is virtually all new in the combinations I am taking up in this book), we need to be in a continuous learning mode.

Educational reform has been painfully slow, but if out of frustration we use technology to end-run the teacher, we will be casting students adrift in the stratosphere. All evidence indicates that students won't learn well if left on their own. Neither will teachers. Speaking of role flipping, students will be great technology teachers for the adults—what a fantastic resource to help bond the new partnership.

Let's redefine the role of teachers and equip them to be the orchestrators of learning and change agents required for learning to flourish. Use the world as the classroom. Embrace ubiquitous technology. For reasons stated throughout this book—essence as easy, the new pedagogy, mind-boggling technology—the time has never been more propitious. Bold moves have a real chance of connecting with what makes humans tick: the appetite for learning and doing something meaningful by collaborating with others. Failure to act is to leave dispirited teachers and students at the mercy of dominant technologies. Without the capacity building of professional capital, it will be no contest.

Fifth, with empathy and capacity building as powerful change resources, *contagion* makes rapid change a reality. Teaching behind the classroom door is about as contagious as a corpse. The iPad did not go viral just because it is a great innovation, but rather because of social networking. Even your grandparents can't avoid becoming addicted.

Our change knowledge sees and uses social contagion as a prime strategy. Remember the ITL findings. Innovative teaching and learning was found sprinkled across schools but was not embedded within many schools or systems. If you want an accelerated strategy to change this situation, *use the group*. Thus figure out how these innovative teachers who are further down the line than their colleagues can be deployed systemically as change agents for other teachers. This is what the Badiliko project does in sub-Saharan Africa, where lead teachers are trained as "digital ambassadors" and reach out to other teachers to improve access to and use of digital resources for learning.[38]

Strategic use of peers is the very finding that the McKinsey group arrived at when they studied 20 educationally successful regions or countries around the world. Some of these systems had gone from poor to adequate; others, from adequate to good to great to excellent. What the McKinsey team concluded was that as the capacity of the teachers increased in systems, *peers became the greatest source of innovation.*[39] Leadership is still critical, but it operates in the service of social contagion. Social capital is the new resource.

Sixth, *transparency* is not voyeurism. It's participating with others to create and assess new things. We have used to great advantage transparency of results and transparency of practice, but it has to be characterized by non-judgmentalism (otherwise people cover up) and collaboration. You get plenty of accountability in the bargain.

Seventh, another change principle, which is also a design principle, involves relentlessly *stripping away the non-essentials.* We sometimes call the non-essentials "distractors." Distractors are focuses' evil twin. There are so many non-essentials in education reform that we could save ourselves a fortune and heaps of grief if we could substantially reduce them.

I named four of the big non-essentials as "wrong drivers" in a 2011 paper.[40] *External accountability* represents a huge cost and doesn't work—there are better and cheaper ways to get more authentic internal accountability. *Individualistic solutions*—more heroic teachers and school principals—is another time and money waster. Instead, develop the group—social capital—and you will do a better job of developing individuals on a large scale. *Technology* was my third "wrong driver" because it is miscast in a starring role instead of an accelerating one. Technology has just as much evil or good as we want to put into it. That is why we need pedagogy and the moral imperative to be the key drivers. Then you can't avoid wanting to embrace technology as one of the best means around. *Ad hoc versus systemic policies* and corresponding strategies was my fourth wrong driver—silos are stagnant. In dynamically interactive systems the whole is greater than the sum of its parts. Ultimately the eight elements of change knowledge serve as the systemic glue that enables groups to learn. Every one of the eight has cohesive power.

Eighth, leadership needs to become the ultimate cohesive driver. Put one way, the role of leaders is to orchestrate the other seven elements of change knowledge we have just identified. Leaders then must foster in others the capacity to focus, to innovate, to empathize, to learn, to collaborate, to relish transparency, to shed non-essentials, and to develop leadership in themselves and others. Ultimately, everyone becomes a change agent.

Change knowledge makes a difference in your success rate. Given that, use the eight elements from Exhibit 5.1 as a checklist, but think of the change process as a learning proposition. Be guided by a vision, but work with others to steer it into action, validate what you are learning, and accelerate action. Use change knowledge deliberately to understand obstacles and to move beyond them. The skinny of change is just that. It is manageable in most circumstances. It is just like learning. When you are engaged with others doing something meaningful, you can accomplish wonders.

Our challenge is to combine the best of change knowledge with the best of technology and pedagogy. If we can do so, progress in educational transformation will accelerate dramatically because of the synergizing influence among these three forces. Pedagogy, technology, and change knowledge operating in concert will become a powerhouse of learning. Once this happens, technology, we can be sure, will pay more than its share. It will become a dynamic player shaping the future.

Making Technology Pay

Technology has dramatically affected virtually every sector in society that you can think of *except* education. It is shocking to have to say that. Learning, surely the most important human resource in the world, is not benefiting from the greatest technical resource on the planet. It is time that gadget goes to school and schools go to gadget 24/7.

Technology is way too powerful for us not to have a plan. We might as well approach it as if technology were a living phenomenon—at least as alive as a plant or as an avalanche. Who knows, 50 years from now as I implied earlier, it might be legal to marry your robot! Stranger things have happened. In any case, we need to take a systems thinking approach to technology and learn to live with it in balance: to treat it as part of the biosphere.

I mentioned that the proposition is a race *with* not against technology. The same thinking applies to the relationship between technology and teachers. Any country with the mindset that investing in technology will compensate for less than brilliant teachers has it wrong. Never think of technology without worrying about teachers and mentors. It is teachers *with* technology who will make the difference. Students are the third partner. All three are co-essential.

People don't realize how bad the situation is in the U.S. public education system. Being 20th or worse in the world is more than a statistic. Much of the problem is hidden, and it is much worse and worsening more than even most critics realize. It is like having brain cancer and ignoring it. The goal over the next decade—and we can accomplish it—should be to double our learning at half the cost. The integration of technology, pedagogy, and change knowledge makes this goal a real possibility. It may not even be that hard because once some of the processes are unleashed in the right direction, they will have a life of their own. Complexity theory has always been about seeking elegant simplicity, letting loose with a small number of powerful forces, and recognizing and reaping the strange attractors that are generated. But it doesn't have to be even that mysterious: first, the problem.

I've Got Bad News and Worse News

The average performance of systems is not the most important factor; rather, the *gap* between low and high performers is. Health economists Richard Wilkinson and Kate Pickett show us with unequivocal evidence "why more equal societies almost always do better."[1] Inequality in education and economic terms is linked to disturbing numbers for the following in a society: level of trust, mental illness, life expectancy and infant mortality, obesity, children's education performance, teenage births, homicides, imprisonment rates, and more. And not just the poor suffer. All categories of social class from top to bottom in unequal societies are less well off on most indicators of well-being. The United States, as Wilkinson and Pickett show, is one of the most unequal societies among the developed countries.

There is worse news. The problem of inequality is becoming more pronounced and more entrenched decade by decade. Deepening inequality is a societal time bomb. So far, technology has not been our friend (because, as I argue in this book, we have not made it our friend). In *Race Against the Machine*, Erik Brynjolfsson and Andrew McAfee claim that our passive, inertia-like relationship to technology is killing us. Under the label of "creative destruction," they put it this way: "Digital technologies change rapidly, but organizations and skills aren't keeping pace. As a result, millions of people are being left behind. Their incomes and jobs are being destroyed, leaving them worse off in absolute purchasing power than before the digital revolution."[2] While the average income in the United States has increased as measured by GDP, the benefits are not equally distributed. Brynjolfsson and McAfee's data show that from 1983 to 2009 all growth in income was a function of the top 20 percent of the population while the other four-fifths experienced a net *decrease*.

In the near future, say these authors, the losers could be up to 90 percent of the population. The top 1 percent has accounted for 65 percent of all growth since 2002. Capital expenditures are up 26 percent since 2008, while labor costs are flat. Corporate profits are at a 50-year high while income from labor is at a 50-year low. In short, there is an unmistakable and (if left to inertia) irreversible shift from labor to capital (and the wealthy own the capital). If we link this trend to Wilkinson and Pickett's analysis, we couldn't create a more catastrophic stealth bomb if we tried. It is a certainty that no good can come of this for the rich or the poor. The unsustainable environment we are creating is socio-economic as much as environmental. The trend is not purposeful. It is a function of the better off helping themselves: of taking advantage of opportunities because they can, because they have greater access to the combined power of education and technology than the rest of the population. No law states that most people automatically benefit from technological progress.

I've Got a Solution

Before you know it, we will be marking the 100-year anniversary of FDR's inaugural address with more despair than at the height of the Great Depression. Roosevelt said, "No country, however rich, can afford the waste of its human resources. Demoralization caused by vast unemployment is our greatest extravagance. Morally, it is the greatest menace to our social order."[3]

The solution, lurking in the stratosphere we have been examining, is not capital over labor. It is capital *with* labor. This observation leads us inevitably to the integrated trinity that forms the basis of this book. The skinny is simple but powerful. The solution lies in the concentration of the three forces of pedagogy, technology, and change knowledge (Exhibit 6.1). If you want to head off destruction, we need to make it all about learning (the pedagogy part), let technology permeate (the technology part), and engage the whole system (the change part).

Exhibit 6.1 The Solution	
1.	Make it all about learning.
2.	Let technology permeate.
3.	Engage the whole system.

Since long lists don't work for change, it is better to have a core philosophy that is practical and powerful. Practical in that it can serve as a guide to action and powerful in that it yields results far beyond our expectations—it unleashes processes that, if not automatically, easily "cause" good things to happen on a wide scale.

We should do less of spending money on assessment detached from designing learning and more of creating learning experiences that are irresistibly engaging. This is why I have made the primary driver pedagogy, or learning. The first thing to ask is this: "How do we make everything we do about learning?" Literacy and deep learning goals—higher-order skills (and proper literacy is higher order) need to dominate. Creativity, passion, and purpose must also flourish. We can do all this by gradually building a pedagogy where as they get older, students are more and more steeped in real-life problem solving, guided by teachers as change agents or mentors.

Second, we can't make everything we do all about learning if we don't let—indeed, make—technology permeate. We already know that digital power is almost limitless. Technology wants what we want if we work with it. Man against nature never worked, nor will man versus machine. Sustainability has taught us that the only future we have is to make focus, empathy, and harmony our modus operandi. Jeremy Rifkin has called this "the empathic civilization" in which evolution is on our side but only if we help it become established.[4]

Letting technology permeate does not have to be an abstract proposition. The mere act of letting technology loose in schools, as we saw when "gadget went to school" or when the illiterate six-year-old picked up the iPad, would do a lot of good. But we can do much more than that. As we discussed there are innovations under way that combine pedagogy and technology in deep and easy-to-use ways. The idea is to deepen the pool of such innovations (remember: *combine* technology and pedagogy to make for irresistibly engaging experiences). My prediction is that around 2013, the quality and abundance of these types of innovations will explode. Let's not make it hard for them to find their way into the public education system. We need to think of this as using technology to increase human and social capital. The fundamental question: How do we get the most out of our racing technology?

Innovations on the Rise

We will be helped by the continued rapid and deep evolution of innovations. Let's take three examples on the horizon: one is a specific technology; another is a social innovation; and the third consists of the unknown bounty (as well as danger) of future technological innovations.

Before we enter into the three illustrations, here's a word about costs. I have not engaged in any financial analysis in this book, but the underlying assumption is that costs will be reduced while quality and impact increase. Technology becomes more powerful as it becomes less expensive. Many of the pedagogical innovations free up inexpensive labor, so to speak—students do more of the work (but find it engaging), adults are involved in more efficient exchanges, crowd sourcing (in which users, the crowd, sort out quality through feedback and circulation of information) becomes widespread, quality teachers can reach more students, the myriad of free digital resources available on the internet constantly increases, and so on. We should enter this new era with a mindset that large savings are to be had as quality multiplies. The main driver should not be to cut costs; however, per person costs will decline naturally.

Now to the three examples.

Concerning the specific technological example, Lord Puttnam, the great filmmaker and educationist, predicted in a talk to Irish primary principals that voice recognition, now in its infancy, would dominate all aspects of life within a decade.[5] We haven't begun to grasp the ramifications of this unstoppable and soon to become ubiquitous phenomenon.

The second breakthrough as an example is a social innovation. It comes from Daniel George and Catherine and Peter Whitehouse and colleagues in their work on *intergenerativity*, how to bring older people and younger people together "to foster collective wisdom and community health."[6] The phenomenon of intergenerational learning has all the hallmarks of stratosphere. It is steeped in real-life problem solving, teaching young and old alike how to nurture social, civic, and environmental responsibility. It teaches empathy across ages. It is cheap, requiring few new resources. And technology is a natural social solidifier as the young teach the old, and everyone benefits.

The third example is based on the overall certainty that technological innovation will go wild in the next period, but we cannot know what it will specifically bring. As an analogy, we can use what is happening in medicine. Eric Topol, a medical doctor and an expert in this field, calls the phenomenon "the creative destruction of medicine."[7]

Topol documents what he sees as the unprecedented convergence of genomics, wireless sensors, imaging, information systems, mobile connectivity, and social networking. It is beyond the scope of my book to go into details, but consider that in biology alone, scientists are now technically able to map the DNA sequence of every human being to uncover individualized genomic makeup. When imaging and information systems are factored in, we soon get into the unknown territory of predicting and thereby altering—preventing—the onslaught of disease. We need not venture into science fiction to picture, as does Topol, that, in the near future, "we could be listening to [installed] brain chips that were afforded wireless activation through our cell phones on demand to uplift our mood, control our temper, or suddenly become romantic."[8]

Leaving this vision aside, Topol concludes, in essence, that from the creative destruction of medicine, "we will arrive at a knowledge of individuals so fine-grained that we can speak of a science of individuality."[9]

Educators will recognize that this is exactly what "personalization" in learning is aiming for—a way of making learning precise and tailored to the individual on a wide scale, that is, for all. Stratosphere predicts that this is the era we have entered, and more important, because of the explosion of possibilities, we must have our wits about us. Those wits concern a preoccupation with how technology and pedagogy go together to produce the learning experiences and outcomes that encompass the four criteria I introduced in Chapter 4—personal learning that is irresistibly engaging, elegantly efficient, technologically ubiquitous, and steeped in real-life problem solving.

In addition to technological and pedagogical savvy, we will need our third key ingredient: *change knowledge*. Local implementation can thrive if we take an essence as easy approach. In that, as Chapter 3 presents, change really isn't as hard as we thought if we capture people's interest and give them enjoyable, worthwhile experiences. It can thrive if we unleash the power of peers (students and teachers alike) to help one another learn and be even greater if we access intergenerational learning. The source of innovation is peers who are further down the line and people of all ages as they learn from one another. To a large extent, to put it crassly, this is cheap labor. The impact can be mind-blowing as we know from social networking. We need, in short, to flip the role of students and teachers, young and old people, and build strong interconnections inside the new ways of learning.

The other level of change knowledge concerns whole-system policy and strategy. I am not talking about a grand design, but more skinny. It didn't take much for us in Ontario to figure out how to combine assertive system direction with widespread bottom-up participation and ownership (and we barely used the power of technology). My colleagues and I have been working on developing great system capacity for whole-system reform.[10] We will need states, provinces, and countries to become engaged in partnerships with a whole-system agenda. All they have to do is to make sure they steep this work in the combination of technology, pedagogy, and change knowledge. In this sense the state is the unit of change. We are seeing an increasing interest in this agenda—in the holy trinity, if you like—on the part of politicians, policy makers, publishers, and universities. For example, under the auspices of the Council of Chief State School Officers (CCSSO) and sponsored by key education foundations, several states have formed a consortium under the rubric of the Innovation Lab Network to work on this very agenda.[11]

Our change knowledge tells us that we must and can combine specific high-powered innovations and strategies for local implementation with widespread dissemination whereby the whole system becomes engaged. With the help of technology we can go viral on the substance of innovation.

Incidentally, the skinny on lean start-ups (rapid learning cycles) and the power of stratospheric-like solutions will enable developing countries to leapfrog the development timeline, thereby achieving progress with breathtaking alacrity and low cost. But that is the topic for another book.

Technology is not a panacea. Not all technology is good for pedagogy. And great pedagogy can and will exist without technology. We have, however, greatly miscast and underutilized technology's power. When we enlist technology in the service of exploratory learning for all, watch out! On the other hand, if we plod along with standards and assessment using technology only as a prop, we will get what we deserve: a higher level of tedium.

It is time to take the lid off learning. It is all there to be assembled. We know that the right combination of our triad already resonates with frustrated learners and frustrated teachers. It is time, to put it in a dramatically exciting way, to meet each other in the stratosphere where we get twice the learning for half the price. Instead of paying for technology that sits on the shelf, let's change the game. Let's race with the machines. Let's make technology pay! If we figure it out, we will find that technology wants what we want.

Notes

Preface

1. Michael Fullan, *Choosing the Wrong Drivers for Whole System Reform.* Seminar series paper no. 204 (Melbourne, AU: Centre for Strategic Education, 2011).
2. Michael Fullan and Maria Langworthy, *A Rich Seam: How New Pedagogies Are Finding Deep Learning* (London, UK: Pearson, 2014).
3. Michael Fullan and Joanne Quinn, *Coherence: The Right Drivers in Action for Schools, Districts, and Systems* (Thousand Oaks, CA: Corwin Press, 2016).

Chapter 1—The Journey

1. Iain McGilchrist, *The Master and His Emissary: The Divided Brain and the Making of the Western World* (New Haven, CT: Yale University Press, 2009).
2. Ibid., 410.
3. Ibid., 174.

Chapter 2—Technology: Power and Peril

1. My thanks to Peter Senge for sending me the Darwin letter, written May 1, 1881, and appearing in *Life and Letters of Charles Darwin.*
2. Evgeny Morozov, *The Net Delusion: The Dark Side of Internet Freedom* (New York: Perseus Book Group, 2011), xiii.
3. Ibid., 31.
4. Ibid., 70.
5. Ibid., 79–80.
6. Ibid., 96.
7. Eli Pariser, *The Filter Bubble: What the Internet Is Hiding from You* (New York: Penguin Books, 2011), 5.
8. Ibid., 8.
9. Ibid., 15.
10. Somini Sengupta, "Should Personal Data Be Personal?" *New York Times,* February 4, 2012, 7.

11. Lori Andrews, "Facebook Is Using You," *New York Times,* February 4, 2012, 7.

12. Nicholas Carr, *The Shallows: What the Internet Is Doing to Our Brains* (New York: W.W. Norton, 2010), 6.

13. Ibid., 5.

14. Norman Doidge, *The Brain That Changes Itself* (New York: Penguin Books, 2007).

15. Carr, *The Shallows,* 115–16.

16. Winifred Gallagher, *Rapt* (New York: Penguin Books, 2009), 10.

17. Nass, quoted in Carr, *The Shallows,* 142.

18. Maggie Jackson, *Distracted: The Erosion of Attention and the Coming Dark Age* (New York: Prometheus Books, 2008), 13.

19. Clay Shirky, *Cognitive Surplus: Creativity and Generosity in a Connected Age* (New York: Penguin Press, 2010), 14.

20. Kevin Kelly, *What Technology Wants* (New York: Viking, 2010), 173.

21. Ibid., 187.

22. David Sloan Wilson, *Evolution for Everyone* (New York: Delacorte Press, 2007).

23. Kelly, *What Technology Wants,* 352.

24. Ibid., 270.

25. Claudia Goldin and Lawrence Katz, *The Race Between Education and Technology* (Cambridge, MA: Harvard University Press, 2008).

26. Ibid., 303.

27. Michael Fullan, *Choosing the Wrong Drivers for Whole System Reform,* Seminar Series Paper No. 204 (Melbourne, AU: Centre for Strategic Education, 2011), 204.

28. Larry Rosen, *Rewired: Understanding the iGeneration and the Way They Learn* (New York: St Martin's Press, 2010), 29.

29. Ibid., 41.

30. Larry Rosen, *iDisorder: Understanding Our Obsession with Technology and Overcoming Its Hold on Us* (New York: Palgrave Macmillan, 2012).

31. Ibid., 14.

©P

Chapter 3—Pedagogy and Change: Essence as Easy

1. Michael Fullan, *Motion Leadership: The Skinny on Becoming Change Savvy* (Thousand Oaks, CA: Corwin Press, 2010).

2. Phillip Schlechty, *Engaging Students: The Next Level of Working on the Work* (San Francisco: Jossey-Bass, 2011).

3. David S. Yeager and Gregory M. Walton, "Social-Psychological Interventions in Education: They're Not Magic," *Review of Educational Research* 81, no. 2 (2011): 267–301.

4. Ibid., 284.

5. Ontario Ministry of Education, Student Success Strategy, www.edu.gov.on.ca/eng/teachers/studentsuccess/strategy.html.

6. Ontario Ministry of Education, Student Success Teams, http://www.edu.gov.on.ca/morestudentsuccess/teams.html.

7. Teresa Amabile and Steven Kramer, *The Progress Principle: Using Small Wins to Ignite Joy, Engagement and Creativity at Work* (Boston: Harvard Business Review Press, 2011).

8. Ibid., 1.

9. Ibid., 89.

10. Tony Wagner, *Creating Innovators: The Making of Young People Who Will Change the World* (New York: Simon and Schuster, 2012), 32.

11. Ibid., 50.

12. Ibid., 107.

13. Ibid., 142.

14. Ken Robinson, *Out of Our Minds: Learning to Be Creative* (Westford, MA: Courier Westford, 2011), 205. See also Ken Robinson, *The Element: How Finding Your Passion Changes Everything* (New York: Viking, 2009).

15. Marc Prensky, "The Reformers Are Leaving Our Schools in the 20th Century," in *Digital Natives to Digital Wisdom: Hopeful Essays for 21st Century Learning* (Thousand Oaks, CA: Corwin, 2012), 20. [italics in original].

16. Jonah Lehrer, *Imagine: How Creativity Works* (New York: Houghton Mifflin Harcourt, 2012).

17. Ibid., 17.

18. Ibid., 29–30.

19. Ibid., 30.

20. Ibid., 31 (italics in original).

21. Ibid., 143.

22. Ibid., 231.

23. Daniel Goleman, Lisa Bennett, and Zenobia Barlow, *Ecoliterate: How Educators Are Cultivating Emotional, Social, and Ecological Intelligence* (San Francisco: Jossey-Bass, 2012).

24. Clayton Christensen and Michael Raynor, *The Innovator's Solution: Creating and Sustaining Successful Growth* (Boston: Harvard Business School Press, 2003).

25. Quaglia Institute, *My Voice* National Student Report (Grades 6–12) 2011 (Portland, OR: Quaglia Institute, 2012).

26. Marc Prensky, *From Digital Natives to Digital Wisdom* (Thousand Oaks, CA: Corwin, 2012), 60.

27. MetLife, *The MetLife Survey of the American Teacher: Teachers, Parents, and the Economy* (New York: MetLife, 2012). www.metlife.com/assets/cao/contributions/foundation/american-teacher/MetLife-Teacher-Survey-2011.pdf.

28. Prensky, "The Reformers Are Leaving," 30.

29. Ibid., 16.

Chapter 4—Digital Disappointments and Dreams

1. Bernie Trilling and Charles Fadel, *21st Century Skills: Learning for Life in Our Times* (San Francisco: Jossey-Bass, 2009).

2. Government of Alberta, *Inspiring Action on Education* (Edmonton: Alberta Education, 2010).

3. Michael Fullan and Nancy Watson, *The Slow Road to Higher Order Skills* (San Francisco: Report to the Stupski Foundation, 2010).

4. Cisco-Intel-Microsoft, *Assessment and Teaching of 21st Century Skills* (Melbourne, AU: ATC21S, 2010).

5. Babette Moeller and Tim Reitzes, *Integrating Technology with Student-Centered Learning* (Quincy, MA: Nellie Mae Education Foundation, 2011).

6. Valerie Steeves, *Young Canadians in a Wired World—Phase III: Teachers' Perspectives* (Ottawa: Media Awareness Network, 2012), 1.

7. Ibid., 16.

8. Juho Matti Norrena, Marja Kankaanranta, and Arto Kalevi Aho-nen, "Innovative Teaching in Finland" (Paper presented at the Annual Meeting of the American Educational Research Association, Vancouver, BC, April 2012), 11.

9. Marc Prensky, "Khan Academy," *Educational Technology* (July–August 2011): 3.

10. Ibid., 3.

11. Michael F. Young et al., "Our Princess Is in Another Castle: A Review of Trends in Serious Games for Education," *Review of Education Research* 82, no. 1 (2012): 61–89.

12. Ibid., 61.

13. Jessica Millstone, *Teacher Attitudes about Digital Games in the Classroom* (New York: Joan Ganz Cooney Center at Sesame Workshop, 2012).

14. John Watson, et al., *Keeping Pace with K–12 Online Learning: An Annual Review of Policy and Practice* (Durango, CO: Evergreen Education Group, 2011). www.evergreengroup.com.

15. John Hattie, *Visible Learning: A Synthesis of over 800 Meta-analyses Relating to Achievement* (London: Routledge, 2009), 243.

16. Bruce Dixon and Susan Einhorn, *The Right to Learn: Identifying Precedents for Sustainable Change* (Anytime Anywhere Learning Foundation, IdeasLAB, and Maine International Center for Digital Learning, 2011), 13.

17. Jesse Brown, "Gadget Goes to School," *Toronto Life,* (January 2012) 35, 37.

18. Ibid., 35.

19. "All the World's a Game," Special Report: Video Games, *The Economist* (December 10, 2011): 3–12.

20. Ibid., 12.

21. Michael Fullan and Nancy Watson, *Deeper Learning: A Right/Wrong Drivers Perspective* (San Francisco: Report to the Hewlett Foundation, 2011).

22. Bill & Melinda Gates Foundation, *Supporting Students: Investing in Innovation and Quality* (Redmond, WA: Bill & Melinda Gates Foundation, 2011).

©P

23. Microsoft Partners in Learning, *Innovative Teaching and Learning Research* (Redmond, WA: Bill & Melinda Gates Foundation, 2011).

24. Ibid., 33.

25. Ibid., 12.

26. Daphne Koller, "Death Knell for the Lecture: Technology as a Passport to Personalized Learning," *New York Times,* December 5, 2011, D8.

27. Phillip Schlechty, *Engaging Students: The Next Level of Working on the Work* (San Francisco: Jossey-Bass, 2011), 10.

28. John Hattie, *Visible Learning for Teachers: Maximizing Impact on Learning* (London: Routledge, 2012), 24.

29. Marc Prensky, *Teaching Digital Natives: Partners for Real Learning* (Thousand Oaks, CA: Corwin Press, 2010).

30. Ken Schwaber, *Agile Project Management with Scrum* (Redmond, WA: Microsoft Press, 2004), xiii.

31. Ryan Martens, in Peter Senge et al., Developmental Stories (meeting on capacity building, Cambridge, MA, Massachusetts Institute of Technology, April 2012).

32. Tony Wagner, *Creating Innovators: The Making of Young People Who Will Change the World* (New York: Simon and Schuster, 2012), 22–23.

33. Ibid., 52.

34. Sean Tierney, ed. *Innovate! Collective Wisdom from Innovative Schools* (self-published, 2011).

35. Willie Smits, "DeforestACTION," 2011, http://www.ted.com/speakers/willie_smits.html.

36. High Tech High, www.hightechhigh.org/.

37. Park Manor Public School, http://pkm.wrdsb.on.ca. Thanks to Principal James Bond, teacher Liz Anderson, and the staff at Park Manor for their input.

Chapter 5—Design Principles and Change Knowledge

1. Walter Isaacson, *Steve Jobs* (New York: Simon and Schuster, 2011).

2. Ibid., 7.

3. Ibid., 78.

4. Ibid.

5. Ibid., 160.

6. Ibid., 232.

7. Ibid., 337.

8. Ibid., 339.

9. Ibid., 340–41.

10. Jeffrey Kluger, *Simplexity* (New York: Hyperion Books, 2008); Michael Fullan, *Motion Leadership: The Skinny on Becoming Change Savvy* (Thousand Oaks, CA: Corwin Press, 2010).

11. Isaacson, *Steve Jobs*, 343.

12. Ibid.

13. Ibid.

14. Ibid., 393.

15. Ibid., 497–98.

16. Orrin T. Murray and Nicole R. Olcese, "Teaching and Learning with iPads, Ready or Not," *TechTrends* 55, no. 6 (2011): 42–48.

17. David Booth, personal communication, February 2012.

18. Chico Harlan, "In South Korea Classrooms, Digital Textbook Revolution Meets Some Resistance." *Washington Post*, March 24, 2012.

19. David Williamson Shaffer, *How Computer Games Help Children Learn* (New York: Palgrave, 2006).

20. Isaacson, *Steve Jobs*, 509.

21. Ibid.

22. Ibid., 545.

23. Ibid., 527.

24. Ibid., 567.

25. Adrian J. Slywotzky, *Demand: Creating What People Love Before They Know They Want It* (New York: Crown Business, 2011).

26. Ibid., 10.

27. Ibid., 40.

28. Ibid., 176.

29. Ibid., 303.

30. Eric Ries, *The Lean Startup: How Today's Entrepreneurs Use Continuous Innovation to Create Radically Successful Businesses* (New York: Crown Business, 2012), 20.

31. Ibid., 84.

32. Ash Maurya, *Running Lean: Iterate from Plan A to a Plan That Works* (Sebastopol, CA: O'Reilly Media, 2012).

33. Isaacson, *Steve Jobs* 553–554.

34. John Hattie, *Visible Learning: A Synthesis of over 800 Meta-analyses Relating to Achievement* (London: Routledge, 2009), 251.

35. John Hattie, *Visible Learning for Teachers: Maximizing Impact on Learning* (London: Routledge, 2012), 161–62.

36. Lyn Sharratt and Michael Fullan, *Putting FACES on the Data: What Great Leaders Do!* (Thousand Oaks, CA: Corwin Press, 2012).

37. Andy Hargreaves and Michael Fullan, *Professional Capital: Transforming Teaching in Every School* (New York: Teachers College Press, 2012).

38. Joe Lemaron, personal communication with author.

39. Mona Mourshed, Chinezi Chijioke, and Michael Barber, *How the World's Most Improved School Systems Keep Getting Better* (London: McKinsey & Company, 2010).

40. Michael Fullan, *Choosing the Wrong Drivers for Whole System Reform,* Seminar Series Paper No. 204 (Melbourne, AU: Centre for Strategic Education, 2011).

Chapter 6—Making Technology Pay

1. Richard Wilkinson and Kate Pickett, *The Spirit Level: Why More Equal Societies Almost Always Do Better* (London: Penguin Books, 2009).

2. Erik Brynjolfsson and Andrew McAfee, *Race Against the Machine: How the Digital Revolution Is Accelerating Innovation, Driving Productivity, and Irreversibly Transforming Employment and the Economy* (Lexington, MA: Digital Frontier Press, 2011, eBook).

3. Franklin Delano Roosevelt, address of the president delivered by radio from the White House, September 30, 1934, http://www.mhric.org/fdr/chat6.html.

4. Jeremy Rifkin, *The Empathic Revolution: The Race to Global Consciousness in a World of Crisis* (New York: Penguin Books, 2009).

5. Lord Puttnam (Speech to the Irish Primary Principals' Network, Dublin, January 26, 2012).

6. Daniel George, Catherine Whitehouse, and Peter Whitehouse, "A Model of Intergenerativity," *Journal of Intergenerational Relationships* 9, no. 4 (2011): 389–404.

7. Eric Topol, *The Creative Destruction of Medicine: How the Digital Revolution Will Create Better Health Care* (New York: Basic Books, 2012).

8. Ibid., 235.

9. Ibid., 228.

10. Those of us directly working on system capacity include Sir Michael Barber, Carol Campbell, Peter Hill, Sir Ken Robinson, Peter Senge, and the Motion Leadership/Madcap group.

11. Council of Chief State School Officers, The Next Generation Learners (Washington, DC: CCSSO, 2011).

Bibliography

"All the World's a Game." Special Report: Video Games, *The Economist*, December 10, 2011.

Amabile, Teresa, and Steven Kramer. *The Progress Principle: Using Small Wins to Ignite Joy, Engagement and Creativity at Work*. Boston: Harvard Business Review Press, 2011.

Andrews, Lori. "Facebook Is Using You." *New York Times*, February 4, 2012, 7.

Brown, Jesse. "Gadget Goes to School." *Toronto Life*, January 2012.

Brynjolfsson, Erik, and Andrew McAfee. *Race Against the Machine: How the Digital Revolution Is Accelerating Innovation, Driving Productivity, and Irreversibly Transforming Employment and the Economy*. Lexington, MA: Digital Frontier Press, 2011. eBook.

Carr, Nicholas. *The Shallows: What the Internet Is Doing to Our Brains*. New York: W.W. Norton, 2010.

Christensen, Clayton, and Michael Raynor. *The Innovator's Solution: Creating and Sustaining Successful Growth*. Boston: Harvard Business School Press, 2003.

Cisco-Intel-Microsoft. *Assessment and Teaching of 21st Century Skills*. Melbourne, AU: ATC21S, 2010.

Council of Chief State School Officers. *The Next Generation of Learners*. Washington, DC: Council of Chief State School Officers, 2011.

Dixon, Bruce, and Susan Einhorn. *The Right to Learn: Identifying Precedents for Sustainable Change*. Anytime Anywhere Learning Foundation, IdeasLAB, and Maine International Center for Digital Learning, 2011.

Doidge, Norman. *The Brain That Changes Itself*. New York: Penguin Books, 2007.

Fullan, Michael. *Motion Leadership: The Skinny on Becoming Change Savvy*. Thousand Oaks, CA: Corwin Press, 2010.

Fullan, Michael. *Choosing the Wrong Drivers for Whole System Reform*. Seminar Series Paper No. 204. Melbourne, AU: Centre for Strategic Education, 2011.

Fullan, Michael, David Devine, Greg Butler, Claudia Cuttress, Mark Hand, Richard Mozer, and Lyn Sharratt. "Motion Leadership/Madcap." Unpublished paper, Toronto, 2011.

Fullan, Michael, and Maria Langworthy. *A Rich Seam: How New Pedagogies Are Finding Deep Learning*. London, UK: Pearson, 2014.

Fullan, Michael, and Joanne Quinn. *Coherence: The Right Drivers in Action for Schools, Districts, and Systems*. Thousand Oaks, CA: Corwin Press, 2016.

Fullan, Michael, and Nancy Watson. *The Slow Road to Higher Order Skills*. San Francisco: Report to the Stupski Foundation, 2010.

Fullan, Michael, and Nancy Watson. *Deeper Learning: A Right/Wrong Drivers Perspective*. San Francisco: Report to the Hewlett Foundation, 2011.

Gallagher, Winifred. *Rapt*. New York: Penguin Books, 2009.

Bill & Melinda Gates Foundation. *Supporting Students: Investing in Innovation and Quality*. Redmond, WA: Bill & Melinda Gates Foundation, 2011.

George, Daniel, Catherine Whitehouse, and Peter Whitehouse. "A Model of Intergenerativity." *Journal of Intergenerational Relationships* 9, no. 4 (2011): 389–404.

Goldin, Claudia, and Lawrence Katz. *The Race Between Education and Technology*. Cambridge, MA: Harvard University Press, 2008.

Goleman, Daniel, Lisa Bennett, and Zenobia Barlow. *Ecoliterate: How Educators Are Cultivating Emotional, Social, and Ecological Intelligence*. San Francisco: Jossey-Bass, 2012.

Government of Alberta. *Inspiring Action on Education*. Edmonton: Alberta Education, 2010.

Hargreaves, Andy, and Michael Fullan. *Professional Capital: Transforming Teaching in Every School*. New York: Teachers College Press, 2012.

Harlan, Chico. "In South Korea Classrooms, Digital Textbook Revolution Meets Some Resistance." *Washington Post*, March 24, 2012.

Hattie, John. *Visible Learning: A Synthesis of over 800 Meta-analyses Relating to Achievement*. London: Routledge, 2009.

Hattie, John. *Visible Learning for Teachers: Maximizing Impact on Learning*. London: Routledge, 2012.

Isaacson, Walter. *Steve Jobs*. New York: Simon & Schuster, 2011.

Jackson, Maggie. *Distracted: The Erosion of Attention and the Coming Dark Age*. New York: Prometheus Books, 2008.

Kelly, Kevin. *What Technology Wants*. New York: Viking, 2010.

Kluger, Jeffrey. *Simplexity*. New York: Hyperion Books, 2008.

Koller, Daphne. "Death Knell for the Lecture: Technology as a Passport to Personalized Education." *New York Times*, December 5, 2011, D8.

Lehrer, Jonah. *Imagine: How Creativity Works*. New York: Houghton Mifflin Harcourt, 2012.

Maurya, Ash. *Running Lean: Iterate from Plan A to a Plan That Works*. Sebastopol, CA: O'Reilly Media, 2012.

McGilchrist, Iain. *The Master and His Emissary: The Divided Brain and the Making of the Western World*. New Haven, CT: Yale University Press, 2009.

MetLife, *The MetLife Survey of the American Teacher: Teachers, Parents, and the Economy*. New York: MetLife, 2012. www.metlife.com/assets/cao/ contributions/foundation/american-teacher/MetLife-Teacher-Survey-2011.pdf.

Microsoft Partners in Learning. *Innovative Teaching and Learning Research*. Redmond, WA: Bill & Melinda Gates Foundation, 2011.

Millstone, Jessica. *Teacher Attitudes about Digital Games in the Classroom*. New York: Joan Ganz Cooney Center at Sesame Workshop, 2012.

Moeller, Babette, and Tim Reitzes. *Integrating Technology with Student-Centered Learning*. Quincy, MA: Nellie Mae Education Foundation, 2011.

Morozov, Evgeny. *The Net Delusion: The Dark Side of Internet Freedom*. New York: Perseus Book Group, 2011.

Mourshed, Mona, Chinezi Chijioke, and Michael Barber. *How the World's Most Improved School Systems Keep Getting Better*. London: McKinsey & Company, 2010.

Murray, Orrin T., and Nicole R. Olcese. "Teaching and Learning with iPads, Ready or Not." *TechTrends* 55, no. 6 (2011): 42–48.

Ontario Ministry of Education. Student Success Strategy. www.edu.gov.on.ca/ eng/teachers/studentsuccess/strategy.html.

Ontario Ministry of Education. Student Success Teams. http://www.edu.gov. on.ca/morestudentsuccess/teams.html.

Norrena, Juho Matti, Marja Kankaanranta, and Arto Kalevi Ahonena. "Innovative Teaching in Finland." Paper presented at the Annual Meeting of the American Educational Research Association, Vancouver, BC, April 2012.

Pariser, Eli. *The Filter Bubble: What the Internet Is Hiding from You*. New York: Penguin Books, 2011.

Prensky, Marc. *Teaching Digital Natives: Partners for Real Learning.* Thousand Oaks, CA: Corwin Press, 2010.

Prensky, Marc. "Khan Academy." *Educational Technology,* July–August 2011.

Prensky, Marc. "The Reformers Are Leaving Our Schools in the 20th Century." In *Digital Natives to Digital Wisdom: Hopeful Essays for 21st Century Learning.* Thousand Oaks, CA: Corwin, 2012. (Also online at http://www. marcprensky.com/writing/+Prensky-The_Reformers_Are_Leaving_Our_ Schools_in_the_20th_Century-please_distribute_freely.pdf.)

Quaglia Institute. *My Voice* National Student Report (Grades 6–12) 2011. Portland, OR: Quaglia Institute, 2012.

Ries, Eric. *The Lean Startup: How Today's Entrepreneurs Use Continuous Innovation to Create Radically Successful Businesses.* New York: Crown Business, 2012.

Rifkin, Jeremy. *The Empathic Revolution: The Race to Global Consciousness in a World of Crisis.* New York: Penguin Books, 2009.

Robinson, Ken. *The Element: How Finding Your Passion Changes Everything.* New York: Viking, 2009.

Robinson, Ken. *Out of Our Minds: Learning to Be Creative.* Westford, MA: Courier Westford, 2011.

Rosen, Larry. *Rewired: Understanding the iGeneration and the Way They Learn.* New York: St Martin's Press, 2010.

Rosen, Larry. *iDisorder: Understanding Our Obsession with Technology and Overcoming Its Hold on Us.* New York: Palgrave, 2012.

Schlechty, Phillip. *Engaging Students: The Next Level of Working on the Work.* San Francisco: Jossey-Bass, 2011.

Schwaber, Ken. *Agile Project Management with Scrum.* Redmond, WA: Microsoft Press, 2004.

Sengupta, Somini. "Should Personal Data Be Personal?" *New York Times,* February 4, 2012, 7.

Shaffer, David Williamson. *How Computer Games Help Children Learn.* New York: Palgrave, 2006.

Sharratt, Lyn, and Michael Fullan. *Putting FACES on the Data: What Great Leaders Do!* Thousand Oaks, CA: Corwin Press, 2012.

Shirky, Clay. *Cognitive Surplus: Creativity and Generosity in a Connected Age.* New York: Penguin Press, 2010.

Slywotzky, Adrian J. *Demand: Creating What People Love Before They Know They Want It*. New York: Crown Business, 2011.

Smits, Willie. "DeforestACTION." 2011. http://www.ted.com/speakers/willie_smits.html.

Steeves, Valerie. *Young Canadians in a Wired World—Phase III: Teachers' Perspectives*. Ottawa: Media Awareness Network, 2012.

Tierney, Sean, ed. *Innovate!: Collective Wisdom from Innovative Schools*. Self-published, 2011.

Topol, Eric. *The Creative Destruction of Medicine: How the Digital Revolution Will Create Better Health Care*. New York: Basic Books, 2012.

Trilling, Bernie, and Charles Fadel. *21st Century Skills: Learning for Life in Our Times*. San Francisco: Jossey-Bass, 2009.

Wagner, Tony. *Creating Innovators: The Making of Young People Who Will Change the World*. New York: Simon and Schuster, 2012.

Watson, John, Amy Murin, Lauren Vashaw, Butch Gemin, and Chris Rapp. *Keeping Pace with K–12 Online Learning: An Annual Review of Policy and Practice*. Durango, CO: Evergreen Education Group, 2011. www.evergreenedgroup.com.

Wilkinson, Richard, and Kate Pickett. *The Spirit Level: Why More Equal Societies Almost Always Do Better*. London: Penguin Books, 2009.

Wilson, David Sloan. *Evolution for Everyone*. New York: Delacorte Press, 2007.

Yeager, David S., and Gregory M. Walton, "Social-Psychological Interventions in Education: They're Not Magic." *Review of Educational Research* 81, no. 2 (2011): 267–301.

Young, Michael F., Stephen Slota, Andrew B. Cutter, Gerard Jalette, Greg Mullin, Benedict Lai, Zeus Simeoni, Mathew Tran, and Mariya Yukhymenko. "Our Princess Is in Another Castle: A Review of Trends in Serious Games for Education." *Review of Education Research* 82, no. 1 (2012): 61–89.

Index

ONTARIO
PRINCIPALS'
COUNCIL
Exemplary Leadership in Public Education

The Ontario Principals' Council (OPC) is a voluntary professional association that represents the interests of principals and vice-principals in Ontario's publicly funded school system. Currently, OPC represents more than 5,000 practising school leaders in elementary and secondary schools as well as over 600 Associates from within the education community.

We believe that exemplary leadership results in outstanding schools and improved student achievement. To this end, we foster quality leadership through world-class professional services and supports. As an ISO 9001 registered organization, we are committed to "quality leadership—our principal product."